MUSIC PERIODICAL LITERATURE:

An Annotated Bibliography of
Indexes and Bibliographies

by

JOAN M. MEGGETT

The Scarecrow Press, Inc.
Metuchen, N.J. & London
1978

Library of Congress Cataloging in Publication Data

Meggett, Joan M   1909-
  Music periodical literature.

  Bibliography: p.
  Includes indexes.
  1. Music--Periodicals--Bibliography. 2. Music--
Periodicals--Indexes--Bibliography. I. Title.
ML128.P24M43   016.78'05   77-19120
ISBN 0-8108-1109-X

PREFACE

Intended primarily for college and university music students as an aid to their research through music periodical literature, this bibliographical work, I trust, will also help to meet the needs of music reference librarians and generally assist researchers to locate periodical articles on music through the fields of the humanities and of the social sciences, both historically and systematically. The work is an outgrowth and greatly enlarged revision of a five-page annotated list, "Periodical Literature on Music," which I compiled in the mid-1950's for the use of students in the course I taught for several years in the School of Music, University of Southern California. It served eventually as a complementary volume to the required text, Vincent Duckles's Music Reference and Research Materials. The author acknowledges with sincere thanks the great help of colleagues, Dr. Vincent Duckles and Dr. Ruth Watanabe. Their respective books have been of inestimable value to me in compiling the book.

CONTENTS

INTRODUCTION

As an integral part of a reference library the importance of periodical articles is recognized. The older volumes in particular provide a priceless record of past ideas and events. All of these would be buried if it were not for available indexes.

Other than the general ones, periodical indexes have, up to 1949, been sadly lacking for music literature. Nearly every other professional field has an index of its own periodical literature; to name a few, Art, Drama, Catholic, Education, Engineering, Psychology, History, Literature, Religion.

The few available indexes for music literature, retrospectively speaking, are incomplete, cover only a short period of time, often for specific fields of music. The most useful are the Schmieder Bibliographie des Musikschrifttums (#123R), 1936-1939; 1950- , but this was suspended from 1940 to 1949, and the latest volume covers only to 1967 (published in 1974); and the old German indexes, ZfMW (#295R), 1918-1935, and ZIM (#294R), 1899-1914. Both have recently been reprinted.

Other indexes appearing before 1949 are Blom (#135R), 1915-1925 (but the majority are only English magazines); Krohn (#206R), 1863-1951 (history of music); Aber (#109), 1700-1922 (German magazines mostly), and a few others limited to only one periodical. The Music Index (1949-) is an indispensable tool, but it is at present over a year in arrears and the last cumulation is 1972!

In the 1930's several attempts were undertaken to remedy this situation. One was the American Periodical Index (#30R), which included some music periodicals published before 1850, but is difficult to use, and is available only in Readex-Microprint form. The most ambitious was sponsored by the Newberry Library in Chicago, with the Music Library

Association Committee on Periodical Indexing enlisting the
help of the Works Progress Administration. The project was
to index 175 recommended music periodicals from the period
1792-1935 (later increased to 1744-1936). By March 1942,
350,000 cards had been compiled and here it stopped. Many
have wanted to carry it on but "the consensus is that revision is not practical." As far as I know, it is now on file
at De Pauw University in Indiana.

In 1963 a questionnaire was sent to members of the
Music Library Association asking for opinions on a one-vol-
ume retrospective index covering the years 1940-1948. It
would seem that this excellent idea did not get off the ground.
Probably too expensive!

Owing then to the dearth of music periodical indexes
prior to the beginning date of the Music Index, there is some
emphasis on retrospective indexing both in music and non-
musical periodical indexes and bibliographies. By adding
"R" to the numbered entries throughout this volume, this is
brought out.

Methodology used: Materials checked and included are
all available general and specialized music and non-music
periodical indexes and bibliographies with sufficient coverage
of articles on music literature; at least ninety-nine per cent
of all works were examined--in the few instances where
perusal was unavailable, a review is quoted--some were examined for music periodical coverage through a recent volume, a cumulated volume, or spot-checking three or more
volumes, early and current issues; if no music periodicals
have been indexed in a particular monograph, but there is a
subject heading under MUSIC, subjects are noted. Synopses
or abstracts of an article on music aid the research worker
immeasurably in determining whether to read the entire article. Most of the abstracting services provide subject and
author indexes and are customarily issued in cumulative volumes. Those which I felt had sufficient music articles to
include are: nos. 39, 42, 56R, 62, 66R, 73R, 92, 97R,
100, and of course the only abstracting service yet published
for music literature, the very excellent RILM Abstracts,
which did not begin until 1967 and is still somewhat behind-
hand.

Subjects covered selectively: A small number of bio-
bibliographical books, which may call attention to similar
bibliographies; some general and specialized or period his-
tories of music, if they contain a comprehensive bibliography

with many articles--Grout's Short History of Opera (179R)
is a well-known example with its over 180 pages of bibliography on the subject of Opera; "Music in Periodicals" is almost
a topic in itself--only nine references were included but they
were important; a few related disciplines such as Dance, Ballet, Folklore, Anthropology (when allied to ethnomusicology)
and references to JAAC, JAF, SFQ were checked.   Both
Jazz and Ethnomusicology have seen a vigorous growth in
recent years and have numerous bibliographical studies--the
principal references were included.

On the annotations: They are essentially descriptive,
outlining the coverage, organization, unique features, etc.,
and listing which and how many music periodicals were indexed.   The abbreviations used for music periodicals are
standard ones.   Otherwise they are spelled out completely.

There is interest and much fascination with the history
of music periodicals both in general and in the United States.
Parts I and II provide a short bibliography on the subject.
Part III covers general non-musical indexes and bibliographies, and Part IV those which are subject oriented.   Part
V includes a variety of fields within the field of music,
brought out through the Subject Index.   The bibliography of
lists of music periodicals in Part VI points out to musicians
the resources of such general reference works as Ulrich's
(#331R) and the important Union List of Serials (#332R) with
its successor New Serial Titles (#323R).   A most comprehensive and interesting list is found in Die Musik in Geschichte
und Gegenwart (#322R), known familiarly as the MGG.

Part I

HISTORY OF MUSIC PERIODICALS (GENERAL)

1(R) Apel, Willi, ed. Harvard Dictionary of Music. 2d
      ed., rev. & enl. Cambridge, Massachusetts:
      Belknap Press of Harvard University, 1969. 935p.
      Under "Periodicals, music" section I: Histori-
      cal survey--a short account of the earliest music
      periodicals, 1735-1770, and the most important
      periodicals thereafter in the 19th century.

2(R) Fellinger, Imogen. Verzeichnis der Musikzeitschrif-
      ten des 19. Jahrhunderts. (Studien zur Musik-
      geschichte des 19. Jahrhunderts, Bd. 10.) Regens-
      burg: Gustav Bosse, 1968. 557p. NACHTRAGEN:
      Folge 1, FAM, 17/1/2, 1970, pp. 7-8; Folge 2,
      FAM, 18/1/2, 1971, pp. 59-62; Folge 3, FAM,
      19/1/2, 1972, pp. 41-44; Folge 4, FAM, 20/3,
      1973, pp. 108-11; Folge 5, FAM, 21/1/2, 1974,
      pp. 36-38; Folge 6, FAM, 23/2, 1976, pp. 62-66.
      List, by date of founding, of 2,305 musical
      journals which began publication between 1798 and
      1918. Locations are given in over 450 libraries in
      thirty-one countries, including British and Ameri-
      can libraries. Complete bibliographical informa-
      tion is given, but no descriptive annotations. The
      Introduction sketches the development of periodicals
      primarily devoted to music. Indexes: Title,
      Editor, Place of Publication, Publisher and Print-
      er, Sources for Listings of Journals Not Found in
      Any Library.

3(R) Freystätter, Wilhelm. Die musikalischen Zeitschriften
      seit ihrer Entstehung bis zur Gegenwart. München:
      T. Riedel, 1884. Reprint: Amsterdam: Frits
      A. M. Knuf, 1963. 139p.
      Based on E. Gregoir's Recherches Historiques
      Concernant les Journaux de Musique, Antwerp:
      1872. Chronological listing from 1722-1884, anno-

1

tated, invaluable in its day as a source of information on the history of music periodicals.   Still
a useful tool, it has been partly supplemented by
Rohlfs (#12R)

4(R)   Grove, Sir George, ed.   Grove's Dictionary of Music
and Musicians.   5th ed., ed. by Eric Blom.   London: Macmillan; New York: St. Martin's Press,
1954.   9 vols.   Supplement, vol. 10, 1961.
Under "Periodicals," vol. 6, pp. 637-72, Section I: Sources and bibliographical notes, many of
which are critically annotated.   Section IV: Historical and critical summary; the beginnings of music periodicals in the 18th century, listed under
country.   Corrections and additions in vol. 10, pp.
344-7.

5(R)   Kahl, Willi und Luther, Wilhelm-Martin.   Repertor-
ium der Musikwissenschaft: Musikschrifttum,
Denkmäler und Gesamtausgaben in Auswahl (1800-
1950) mit Besitzvermerken deutscher Bibliotheken
und musikwissenschaftlicher Institute.   Kassel:
Bärenreiter, 1953.   271p.
Under "Zeitschriften" lists 187 music periodicals
from 1800-1950, including yearbooks, in all European languages, with their locations in postwar
German libraries.   They were selected for their
musicological importance.

6(R)   Kidson, Frank.   "English Magazines Containing Music, Before the Early Part of the 19th Century."
MA, 3 (January 1912), 99-102.
Chronological list of twenty-four magazines,
from the Gentleman's Journal, 1692-1694, to Walker's Hiberian Magazine, 1771-1811, which contained
music.

7(R)   Lawrence, W. J.   "18th-Century Magazine Music."
MA, 3 (October 1911), 18-39.
Music in the supplements of 18th-century maga-
zines, which included songs sung in the pleasure
gardens, the playhouse and the concert-room, airs,
tunes, country dances.   From Exshaw's London
Magazine, May 1741-1794, Dublin: chronological
list, 1743-1794, with 350 items and annotations.
Printed for Edward Exshaw at the Bible on Cork
Hill, over against the Old Exchange.   In 1911, it

was located in the National Library, Royal Irish
Academy, the Library of Trinity College, Dublin.

8(R) Moser, Hans Joachim. Musik Lexikon. 4. , stark
      erweiterte Aufl. Hamburg: H. Silorski, 1955. 2
      vols.
            Under "Zeitschriften," pp. 1452-54, chronolog-
      ical list from the 18th century of music periodicals.

9(R) Die Musik in Geschichte und Gegenwart. Ed. by
      Friedrich Blume. Kassel: Bärenreiter, 1949- .
      15 vols. with Suppl.
            Under "Zeitschriften," vol. 14, columns 1041-
      1188, 1968: history of music periodicals and seri-
      al publications from the 18th century to the period
      between World War I and II. Compiled by Imogen
      Fellinger.

10(R) O'Meara, Eva J. "Music in 17th- and 18th-Century
       Periodicals in the Yale University Library."
       NOTES, ser. 1, n. 2 (December 1934), 1-6.
             Over forty-five non-musical periodicals were
       checked, including French and German serials to
       1800 classed as General Periodicals with a few
       German sets classed as Literature. Some Latin,
       Dutch, and English journals are also listed. They
       were checked with the following in mind: adver-
       tisements or reviews of music; music in articles on
       other subjects; actual music (a page or two in-
       serted); performances (in the Bibliothèque Britan-
       nique for 1740 is a list, by years, of all the op-
       eratic works performed in England from 1566 to
       1655).

11(R) Prod'homme, Jacques G.   "Essai de Bibliographie
       des Périodiques Musicaux de Langue Française."
       Société Française de Musicologie Bul. , 1/2 (May
       1918), 76-90.
             Chronological list, by century, 18th to 20th. Divi-
       sions: Paris--Journaux et Revues de Province;
       Journaux et Revues en Langue Française Publiés à
       étranger, 18th-19th. Useful list but dates are bad-
       ly incomplete.

12(R) Rohlfs, Eckart. Die deutschsprachigen Musikperiodica,
       1945-1957. (Forschungsbeiträge zur Musikwissen-
       schaft, 11.) Regensburg: Gustav Bosse, 1961.

108p.
Dissertation, Ph.D., University of Munich, 1957.
First section, pp. 1-108, with eleven pages of
graphic tables, gives facts of music journals in
Germany. For example, table 2 shows the growth
of music periodicals from almost none in 1945 to
over 250 in 1957. A survey of music periodicals
from 1685 includes some non-German journals, a
discussion of the music press, a bibliography of
thirty-one books concerning music periodicals,
sources from 1945 (item nos. 51-138): bibliography,
catalog, articles concerning music periodicals, locations and a history of music periodicals after
1945 in twelve categories (see #327R).

13(R)   Thoumin, Jean Adrien.   Bibliographie Retrospective
        des Périodiques Français de Littérature Musicale,
        1870-1954.   Paris: Éditions Documentaires In-
        dustrielles et Techniques, 1957.   179p.
            Preface by Madame Elizabeth Lebeau (Biblio-
        thèque Nationale). Approximately 600 French mu-
        sic periodicals listed, with a chronological index,
        pp. 85-150, and an index of proper names, asso-
        ciations, societies, countries, geographical. In-
        cludes the location of the library holding the peri-
        odical in a summary of the bibliographic sources
        used.

Part II

HISTORY OF MUSIC PERIODICALS
IN THE UNITED STATES

14(R) American Periodical Collection: American Periodicals
       I, 18th Century; American Periodicals II, 1800-
       1850; American Periodicals III, 1850-1900. Ann
       Arbor, Michigan: Xerox University Microfilms,
       1972- .
       From the Publisher's brochure: Series I is a
       collection of ninety serial titles from 1741-1799,
       thirty reels of 35mm positive microfilm. Musical
       periodicals included: American Musician Magazine,
       May 1786-September 1787, The Musical Magazine,
       no. 1-6, 1792-1801. Series II, about 900 titles,
       1800-1850, on microfilm, with subject matter rang-
       ing from literature and the humanities to the sci-
       ences and social sciences--many are indexed in
       Poole's Index (#37R); fifteen musical periodicals
       included. Series III, 118 titles, 1850-1900, period
       of Civil War and Reconstruction, on microfilm.

15(R) Davison, Sister Mary Veronica. American Music
       Periodicals in the Later Nineteenth Century: 1853-
       1899. Ph.D. , Musicology, University of Minne-
       sota, 1973. 2 vols. 635p.
       Basic information about the music periodicals
       issued in the United States from 1853 through 1899
       with publishers, editors, runs, title changes, con-
       tents and locations of copies; the attitude of Amer-
       ican music journals toward European and American
       artist performers. Nearly 300 journals were ex-
       amined as located in five major libraries.

16(R) Flandorf, Vera. Music Periodicals in the United
       States: A Survey of Their History and Contents.
       Unpublished Master's Thesis (Library Science),
       University of Chicago, 1952. 221p.
       Period division: 1800-1865, 1866-1905, 1906-

1951, with summaries. Discussion of editors, publishers, contributors, etc.; content patterns: size,
price, frequency, music, reviews, article content.
Appendices: Chronological annotated list of music
periodicals (total, 558, about 200 were examined
in detail); Check list of those in the United States,
1787-1951. Listed in Weichlein (#28R) under symbol F with number indicating page on which annotation may be found in thesis.

17(R)   Grimes, Calvin Bernard. American Musical Periodicals, 1819-1852: Music Theory and Thought in
the United States. Ph.D., University of Iowa,
1974. 312p.
Principal objective to determine the state of music theory and thought in the early nineteenth century, those which contain literary material as well
as music. Thirty-four literary American musical
periodicals examined. The first American musical
magazine to contain significant literary materials:
Literary and Musical Magazine, (1819?).

18(R)   Jackson, Bruce, comp. The Negro and His Folklore
in 19th-Century Periodicals. (Bibliographical and
Special Series of the American Folklore Society,
18.) Edited, with an introduction, by Bruce Jackson. Austin, Texas: University of Texas, 1967.
394p.
Chronologically arranged, 1838-1899. Articles
and reviews from 19th-century American periodicals
on Negro folk song, speech, custom, story (non-
musical folklore), a few stage minstrelsy. Periodicals mostly well-known and popular literary
types. One musical periodical included: Dwight's
Journal of Music (four articles). Appendix II/B:
list of articles in JAF, 1888-1901.

19(R)   Johnson, H. Earle. "Early New England Periodicals
Devoted to Music." MQ, 26/2 (April 1940), 153-
61.
Discussion of fifteen periodicals, all but one issued from Boston. Most of these didn't survive a
third year of publication, with the exception of
Dwight's Journal of Music, 1852-1881. One of the
most important was the Boston Musical Gazette,
1846-1848, which gave a complete program of concerts in Boston and a biography of J. S. Bach.

20(R) _____ . "Henry C. Lewis's Musical Magazine."
NOTES, 32/1 (September 1975), 7-14.
   Henry C. Lewis's (his dates unknown) Literary
Museum and Musical Magazine (Philadelphia) be-
came a fully musical periodical which preceded
The Euterpeiad (assumed to be America's earliest
musical periodical), July 1817-June 9, 1820.

21(R) Lowens, Irving. "Writings about Music in the Periodicals of American Transcendentalism (1835-1850)."
JAMS, 10/2 (Summer 1957), 71-85.
   The seven Transcendental periodicals appearing
between 1835 and 1850 are listed in an Appendix:
Aesthetic Papers (1849), Boston Quarterly Review
(1838-1842), The Dial (1840-1844), The Harbinger
(1845-1849), The Western Messenger (1835-1841),
The Spirit of the Age (1849-1850), The Present
(1843-1847). Of these, the most important was
The Harbinger, in which appeared Transcendental-
colored ideas about music.

22(R) Millen, Irene. American Musical Magazines, 1786-
1865. Unpublished Master's Thesis (Library Science), Carnegie Institute of Technology, 1949.
55p.
   "A survey and annotated bibliography of twenty-
six music periodicals, 1786-1865, in the Carnegie
Library of Pittsburgh" (quoted from Flandorf
[#16R]). Followed by the Stephen thesis, 1866-
1886, (#27R). Listed in Weichlein (#28R) under
symbol M with number indicating the page upon
which the annotation may be found in the thesis.

23(R) Mott, Frank Luther. A History of American Magazines. Cambridge, Massachusetts: Harvard University, 1938-1968. 5 vols.
   Includes musical journals in America from 1741-
1930. Vol. 5 sketches twenty-one magazines,
1905-1930, with a cumulative index of all volumes.
Lists and comments on the most and the least important ones which contained music selections, including music criticism, those devoted to the music trade of the time, those which included essays
on opera, songs, concerts, Negro influence in the
Civil War Period, etc. Listed in Weichlein (#28R)
under Mott 3 & 4 (vols. 3 & 4).

24(R) O'Handley, Marie. "Early Music Periodicals in New
       York City. " Listen, 1 (May-June, 1964), 5-7.
          No musical magazine was published in New York
       City before the 19th century; The Lyre, or New
       York Musical Journal, June 1824-May 1825; The
       Euterpeiad: An Album of Music, Poetry and Prose,
       1830-1831--many quotations from these two periodi-
       cals.

25(R) Richardson, Lyon N. A History of Early American
       Magazines, 1741-1789. New York: Thomas Nelson
       & Sons, 1931. 414p.
          Thirty-seven periodicals studied. Music appear-
       ing in a few magazines mentioned: Boston Maga-
       zine, 1784-1786, American Musical Magazine,
       1786-1787, The Columbian Magazine, 1787-1790,
       which was edited in its first few months by Francis
       Hopkinson. One of his songs was printed as an in-
       sert, "Come, Fair Rosina"; in 1789 appeared his
       "The Bud of the Rose. " The Massachusetts Maga-
       zine, 1789-1796, had songs in its first volume and
       some Hopkinson songs.

26(R) Snodgrass, Isabel S. American Musical Periodicals
       of New England and New York, 1786-1850. Unpub-
       lished Master's Thesis, Columbia University Grad-
       uate Library School, 1947. 103p.
          Thirty-three of the early publications are ana-
       lyzed. Divisions: Music periodicals before 1800;
       music periodicals, 1800-1850. Noted: history and
       biography, reviews, instruction, editorials, news,
       criticism, programs, musical supplements, maga-
       zine mortality. Appendices: Checklist of music
       periodicals; Chronological table of New England and
       New York musical periodicals; list of materials con-
       sulted for historical background.

27(R) Stephen, Carol. Descriptive Bibliography of Early
       American Music Periodicals, 1866-1886, in the Car-
       negie Library of Pittsburgh. Unpublished Master's
       Thesis (Library Science), Carnegie Institute of
       Technology, 1954. 55p.
          Follows Millen thesis (#22R). Holdings in the
       Carnegie Library listed in Weichlein (#28R) under
       symbol S, with number indicating page on which an-
       notation may be found in the thesis.

28(R) Weichlein, William J. A Checklist of American Mu-
       sic Periodicals, 1850-1900. (Detroit Studies in
       Music Bibliography, 16.) Detroit: Information Co-
       ordinators, Inc., 1970. 103p.
          List of 309 music periodicals published from
       1850 to 1900 and carried on until 1922. Location
       symbol indicates the library holding a representa-
       tive number of issues. Includes: possible length
       of runs, names of editors, publishers and other
       pertinent information. Does not include: those
       which published only music, program notes for sym-
       phony orchestras, proceedings of associations. Ap-
       pendices: Chronological register of American mu-
       sic periodicals, 1850-1900; Geographical distribu-
       tion. Index of editors and publishers, with item
       number reference to checklist.

29(R) Wunderlich, Charles E. A History and Bibliography
       of Early American Musical Periodicals, 1782-1852.
       Ph.D., University of Michigan, 1962. 783ℓ.
          From the first musical periodical appearing in
       1782 to Dwight's Journal of Music in 1852, in two
       parts: History; Descriptive bibliography of periodi-
       cals collected from author's personal library and
       from about thirty other libraries. There are sixty-
       six entries, which include forty-nine located, four-
       teen unlocated and three misleading titles, all with
       complete descriptive details. Appendices: Index to
       all titles in the chronological bibliography; Geograph-
       ical index to the bibliography; Register-index of
       names, addresses, biographical information of over
       800 publishers, printers, engravers, composers,
       and authors who had connections with music periodi-
       cals before 1852.

Part III

MUSIC PERIODICAL LITERATURE IN GENERAL
NON-MUSIC INDEXES AND BIBLIOGRAPHIES

30(R) American Periodical Index, 1728-1850. Ed. by Nelson F. Adkins. New York: Readex, 1963- .
Available only in Readex-Microprint form. Originally began in 1934 in the English Department of
Washington Square College, with the assistance of
W. P. A. workers under the direction of Oscar Car-
gill. Approximately 650,000 catalog cards were
made and reproduced on 1,144 microprint cards.
With 400 to 500 cards reproduced on each microprint card, the subject MUSIC (with subheadings)
fills seven microprint cards, located in Box F,
cards F 228-234. Entries elsewhere, as those under SONG, have cards indexed under authors, composers, titles, first lines. Mostly hand-written,
by many different hands.

Annual Magazine Subject Index see Cumulated
Magazine Subject Index.

31(R) Bibliographie der fremdsprachigen Zeitschriften-Literatur. Abteilung B, 1911-1924, 1925/26-1964. Leipzig: Felix Dietrich, vols. 1-20; N. F., vols. 1-51,
1911-1924, 1925/26-1962/64.
In 1965 merged with Internationale Bibliographie
der Zeitschriften-Literatur (# 35). Covers about
3,000 non-German periodicals, is particularly strong
in English, French and Italian languages. Important in finding articles in French, owing to the lack
of French periodical indexes. The first series is
a subject index only; the second series has, in addition, an author index. Music periodicals indexed
(1962/64 vol. checked): M&L, MD, MQ, MR, Mus-
Cour, and many others.

32(R) Cotgreave, Alfred, ed., comp. A Contents-Index to
General and Periodical Literature. Ann Arbor,

Michigan: Gryphon Books, 1971. 743p. Facsimile
reprint of the 1900 edition published by Elliot Stock,
London.
Periodicals of the 19th century including some
from the United States. Under subject MUSIC are
headings such as "Music Halls," "Musicians."

33(R)   Cumulated Magazine Subject Index, 1907-1949: A Cumulation of the F. W. Faxon Company's Annual
Magazine Subject Index.... Boston: G. K. Hall,
1964. 2 vols.
Vol. 1, 1907 has the title: Magazine Subject-In-
dex: a Subject Index to Seventy-Nine American and
English Periodicals. No actual music periodicals
indexed, but twenty-three columns devoted to the
subject MUSIC. The 1909 vol. includes as Part II
the Dramatic Index for 1909 (#65R), which continued
until 1923, then was called the Annual Magazine Subject Index to 1949, while the Dramatic Index continued alone, 1924-1949. The last issue, 1949, under
MUSIC, indexed: Folklore (London), JAF, SFQ.

34(R)   Cumulative Index to a Selected List of Periodicals:
Authors, Subjects, Titles, Reviews, Portraits.
Cleveland: Ohio Public Library, 1896-1899. 4
vols.
Under heading MUSIC, p. 242-3, three columns
with cross-references: Church Music, Musical Instruments, National Songs, Opera, Oratorio, Orchestral Music, Songs, etc. Music periodical indexed: Music (Chicago).

35   Internationale Bibliographie der Zeitschriften-Literatur
aus allen Gebieten des Wissens (International Bibliography of Periodical Literature Covering All Fields
of Knowledge). Jahrg. 1- . Hrsg. von Otto Zeller.
Osnabrück: Felix Dietrich, 1963/64- .
Continuation in combined form of Bibliographie
der deutschen Zeitschriftenliteratur (#48R) and Bibliographie der fremdsprachigen Zeitschriftenliteratur (#31R). More than 7,600 periodicals consulted.
Subject index, with separate author index. Under
Subject MUSIC, German catch-words and cross-references dealing with music from English and
French forms.

Magazine Subject Index   see   Cumulated Magazine
Subject Index.

36(R)   Nineteenth-Century Readers' Guide to Periodical Lit-
        erature.   New York: H. W. Wilson, 1890-1899.
        Supplementary index, 1900-1922. New York: H.
        W. Wilson, 1944.   2 vols.
            Author-subject index to fifty-one leading periodi-
        cals of the time.   Authors are identified for many
        articles published anonymously.   Music (or related)
        periodical indexed: JAF.   Under subject MUSIC
        are sub-headings such as: Acoustics and Physics,
        with many cross-references.

37(R)   Poole's Index to Periodical Literature.   Boston:
        Houghton Mifflin, 1891.   1802-1881, rev. ed. , 1891.
        Supplements, 1882-1887, 1887-1892, 1892-1896,
        1897-1902, 1902-January 1, 1907.
            The first periodical index and the forerunner of
        Readers' Guide (# 38R).   Subject index only, with
        American and English periodicals indexed.   Music
        subject headings such as: Music, History of; Music,
        Popular; Music, Church; under individual composers,
        etc.   Music periodicals indexed: Music (Chicago),
        Folklore (London), JAF, Masters in Music (Boston).

38(R)   Readers' Guide to Periodical Literature.   Vol. 1- .
        New York: H. W. Wilson, 1905- .
            Major current guide to about 160 well-known gen-
        eral and non-technical magazines from 1900 to the
        present.   Author and subject index; titles only for
        works of fiction.   Music periodicals indexed: ARG
        (1961-), Etude (to 1957), HSR (1961-), MQ (to
        1953; again March 1968-), MusAmer (to 1964),
        Musician (to 1948), OpN (1961-).   Currently in-
        dexed: ARG, HSR, MQ, OpN.

Part IV

MUSIC PERIODICAL LITERATURE IN SPECIAL
NON-MUSIC INDEXES AND BIBLIOGRAPHIES

39   Abstracts of Folklore Studies. Vol.1- . Philadel-
     phia: University of Pennsylvania, The American
     Folklore Society, January 1963- .
     1,000 abstracts a year of articles in about 100
     periodicals. Deals with folklore in its broadest
     sense--tale, song, proverb, arts and crafts, eth-
     nology. Classified subject arrangement, with an
     author-subject index. Vol.1, no.1 indexes music
     and related periodicals: Folklore and Folk Music
     Archivist; Sing Out!; Tatzil (the Chord): A Form
     for Music Research and Bibliography. Vol.1, no.2
     added: African Music, Autoharp, ETHNO, JAF.
     Vol.8, no.2 added: Studies in Music, Inter-Amer-
     ican Music Bul., Jahrbuch für musikalische Volks-
     und-Völkerkünde, JAMS, M&L, Revista Musical
     Chilena, Sovetskaia Muzka. Vol.9, no.1: MQ,
     MT, etc.

40(R) Acoustical Society of America, Journal. Vol.1- .
     Menasha, Wisconsin: Acoustical Society of Ameri-
     ca, October 1929- .
     Cumulative indexes to vols. 21-30, 1949-1958,
     and vols. 31-35, 1959-1963. Headings under MUSIC:
     Sound-Societies, Musical Acoustics, Architectural
     Acoustics. No actual music periodicals indexed.

41(R) Africa South of the Sahara: Index to Periodical Litera-
     ture, 1900-1970. (U.S. Library of Congress African
     Section) Boston, Massachusetts: G. K. Hall, 1971.
     4 vols. Suppl., Boston: G. K. Hall, 1973- .
     Intended to provide citations to contents of jour-
     nals not covered in the standard guides to periodical
     literature. Arranged by area (region or country)
     and by subject. Vol.1: Africa-General-Central Af-

rica, the section on music has three columns per
page, pp. 212-218; vol. 2:   Central African Republic-
Ivory Coast, no music listed; vol. 3:   Kenya-Soma-
lia, the section on music (on Nigeria), six columns
per page, pp. 328-9; vol. 4:   South Africa-Zambia,
section on music, p. 22 (one citation from MQ), on
music (Tanzania), p. 317.   Music and related periodicals indexed: African Music, The Composer (London), Journal of the Folklore Institute, JIFMC,
Journal of the New African Literature and the Arts,
Jahrbuch für musikalische Volks- und Völkerkünde.

42   African Abstracts: A Quarterly Review of Ethnological
          Social and Linguistic Studies Appearing in Current
          Periodicals.   Vol. 1- .   London: International Af-
          rican Institute, 1950- .
              About 900 abstracts per year, in English, from
          journals in various languages.   Annual general in-
          dex includes an Ethnic and Linguistic index, an
          author index and a list of periodicals abstracted.
          Music subjects include: Dancing, Music, Ivory
          Coast Musicians, Musical Instruments, with cross-
          references to particular instruments cited in the
          article.   Music periodicals indexed: JIFMC, JAF.
          Annotations are in French and in English.

43(R)   Applied Science and Technology Index.   Vol. 1- .
          New York: H. W. Wilson, February 1913- .
              From 1913 to 1957 called Industrial Arts Index.
          Under subject MUSIC: Electronic Music, Acoustics,
          Jazz Music, Tones, Musical Instruments, Music-
          Acoustics and Physics.   Indexes technical and engi-
          neering periodicals which include periodicals related
          to music as: Audio, Audio Engineering Society
          Journal (# 45), Acoustical Society of America, Jour-
          nal (# 40R).

44(R)   Art Index: A Cumulative Author and Subject Index to
          Fine Arts Periodicals and Museum Bulletins Cover-
          ing Archaeology, Architecture, Art History, Arts
          and Crafts, Fine Arts, Graphic Arts, etc.   New
          York: H. W. Wilson, 1929- .
              Music subjects as: Art and Music, Church Mu-
          sic, Bands, Composition (Music), Folk Songs, Jazz,
          Moving Picture Music, Phonograph Records, Rock
          'n' Roll Music, Musicians-Portraits, Music-Manu-
          scripts.   No music periodicals indexed, but related:

Arts and Architecture, International Film Quarterly,
JAAC, RenN, Sight and Sound, etc.

45   Audio Engineering Society, Journal. Vol. 1- . Utica,
        New York: Audio Engineering Society, January
        1953- .
            Subject headings as: Acoustics, Electronic Mu-
        sic, Sound-Recordings and Reproducing. No music
        periodicals indexed.

46   Australian Periodical Index. Vol. 1- . Sydney: Pub-
        lic Library of New South Wales, 1950- .
            Under subjects only, articles are indexed which
        deal with subjects within the sphere of interest:
        Australia, New Zealand, Southwest Pacific and the
        Antarctic. Cumulative volume for 1956-1959 has two
        pages under the subject MUSIC, with many cross-
        references. Music periodical indexed (as noted):
        Canon: Australian Journal of Music.

47(R)   Australian Public Affairs Information Service (APAIS):
        A Subject Index to Current Literature. Canberra:
        National Library of Australia, 1945- .
            Music periodicals indexed (1973): Australian So-
        ciety for Music Education, Australian Journal of
        Music, Music and the Teacher (Victorian Music
        Teachers' Association).

        Avery Index to Architectural Periodicals see
        Columbia University Libraries. Avery Architecture
        Library.

48(R)   Bibliographic Index: A Cumulative Bibliography of
        Bibliographies. New York: H. W. Wilson, 1945-
            Selection for inclusion is made from bibliogra-
        phies which have fifty or more citations, with con-
        centration on Germanic and Romance languages.
        Indexes bibliographies in books, pamphlets, periodi-
        cal articles. Cumulative vol. published in 1945
        covers the years 1937-1942, with eighteen columns
        devoted to music. Cumulations following devote
        four-six columns to music. Music periodicals in-
        dexed (1937-1942): Etude, JAAC, JAF, MQ, MR,
        M&L, MM; later volumes: AMT, JRME, Jahrbuch
        für Liturgik und Hymnologie (#197), Mozart Jahr-
        buch, MusAmer (to 1965), NOTES, etc.

49(R)   Bibliographie der deutschen Zeitschriften Literatur.
        Abteilung A, 1896-1964.   Leipzig: Felix Dietrich,
        1897-1964.   Vols. 1-128.   Erganzunsbände, vols.
        1-20, 1861-1917.
            In 1965, merged with Internationale Bibliographie
        der Zeitschriften-Literatur (# 87R).   Supplement
        covers the years 1861-1895.   Indexed by subject,
        covering only German periodicals.   Under subject
        MUSIK-MUSIKWISSENSCHAFT, vol. 128, 1964:   pp.
        1021-25 in double columns.   Music periodicals in-
        dexed include: Acta Mozartiana, AfMW, AM, AMZ,
        MfMG, Melos, Musik und Kirche, Musikwelt, NMZ,
        NZfM, SIM, ZIM.

50(R)   Biography Index: A Cumulative Index to Biographical
        Material in Books and Magazines.   New York: H.
        W. Wilson, 1946- .
            Indexes biographical material in current books in
        the English language and in about 1, 700 periodicals.
        Includes any type of reference that is biographical
        in character--memoirs, obituaries, etc.   In two
        parts: list of biographees, giving full name, dates,
        nationality and occupational profession (all biogra-
        phees are American unless otherwise indicated);
        classified list of persons by profession or occupa-
        tion.   Music periodicals indexed: AMT, HSR, JAAC,
        JAF, M&L, MQ, MR, MusEdJ, MusJ, MusAmer,
        NOTES, OpN, SchMus.

51(R)   Book Review Digest.   New York: H. W. Wilson,
        1905- .
            Consensus of critical opinion, pros and cons, of
        important reviews appearing in over seventy-five
        magazines; must have been published or distributed
        in the United States.   A work of non-fiction must
        have received two or more reviews, written within
        eighteen months following publication.   At least one
        review must be for a journal published in the United
        States.   Subject and title index.   An abstract of the
        review is given.   Music and related periodicals in-
        dexed: JAAC, MQ, NOTES, Saturday Review.

52   Book Review Index.   Detroit: Gale Research, 1965-
        1968; 1972- .
            Supplements the Book Review Digest (# 51R).
        Policy is to include every review in every periodi-
        cal indexed.   Indexes over 200 periodicals in the

fields of general fiction, non-fiction, humanities,
social sciences, librarianship and bibliography.
Author index gives the author of the review. Music and related periodicals indexed: ARG, JAF,
JAAC, MusEdj, NOTES, OpN, SchMus, Spec, etc.

53   British Education Index. Vol. 1- . Comp. by the
        Librarians of the Institute of Education. London:
        Library Association, August 1954/November 1958-
        Cumulation of the Index to Selected British Edu-
        cational Periodicals. In 1972 it became an annual
        with quarterly issues. Entries from about fifty
        periodicals, extracted from the British Humanities
        Index (#54R), and journals. Under subject MUSIC
        EDUCATION: Music Education and Geography, Mu-
        sic Education and History, Music Education and
        School Worship, with many sub-headings and cross-
        references. Music periodicals indexed include:
        MT, Music in Education.

54(R)   British Humanities Index. London: Library Associa-
        tion, 1962- .
        Supersedes the Subject Index to Periodicals,
        1915-1922, 1926-1961, omitting titles in fields of
        technology, education, business, and the biological
        and medical sciences, which are in part covered
        by two other English publications, the British Tech-
        nology Index (#55) and the British Education Index
        (#53). About 300 British periodicals are indexed
        by subject. Music and related periodicals indexed:
        Chesterian (to 1961), Consort, English Church Mu-
        sic, GSJ, Listener, M&L, MO, MR, MT, Opera
        (London), Organ, PMA, MMR (to Dec. 1960), Tem-
        po, Viola da Gamba Society Bul.

55   British Technology Index. London: Library Associa-
        tion, 1962- .
        28,000 references a year to articles in about
        400 British technical journals, many not covered
        elsewhere. References to music under headings
        as: Music, Scores-Lithography, Musical Instru-
        ments, Tuning, Manufacture, Music-Electronic,
        Music-Computers. No music periodicals indexed.

56   Bulletin Signalétique. Section 19-24: Sciences humai-
        nes: Philosophie. Paris: Centre de Documenta-
        tion, Centre National de la Recherche Scientifique,
        1947- .

Abstracts, in French, of articles from about
3,000 periodicals of the world. Covers the field
of humanities, including Dance, Music, Theatre
Arts. Classified subject arrangement with a separate subject index for each section. Music as a
subject varies in the twenty-two vols. of this set,
more often found in Section 19.

57   Business Periodicals Index. New York: H. W. Wil-
        son, 1958- .
        Subject index to periodicals in the fields of ac-
counting, advertising, banking and finance, general
business, insurance, labor and management, indus-
tries and trades, etc. For material published between 1913 and 1957, the annual and biennial vols.
of Industrial Arts Index may be consulted. Under
subject MUSIC; Copyright--Music, Electronic Data
Processing--Music, Jazz Music, Music in Industry,
Musical Instruments, Radio Processing--Music.
No music periodicals indexed.

58(R)   Canadian Periodical Index (Index de Périodiques Cana-
        diens). Vol. 1- . Ottawa: Canadian Library
        Association, January 1948- .
        From 1948-1963, called Canadian Index to Period-
icals and Documentary Films. Author, subject index to articles in eighty-eight English and French
language magazines published in Canada, many not
indexed elsewhere. Music periodicals indexed:
Archives de Folklore, Canadian Composer, Canadian Music Journal, Performing Arts in Canada.

59(R)   Catholic Periodical and Literature Index: A Cumulative
        Author and Subject Index to a Selected List of Cath-
        olic Periodicals. Vol. 1- . New York: Catholic
        Library Association, 1930.
        Former title: Catholic Periodical Index. Indexes
over 200 periodicals published mainly in the United
States, Canada, England and Ireland. Under MUSIC:
Audio-Visual Education, Church Music, Phonograph
Records, Music--History & Criticism, Music--Re-
ligious Aspects, Musical Instruments, School Music,
etc. Music periodicals indexed include: Listening,
Musart, Sacred Music. (Articles chosen which are
of interest to or by Catholics.)

60(R)   Chicago. Art Institute. Ryerson Library. Index to

Periodicals.   Comp. in the Ryerson Library, Art
Institute of Chicago.   Boston: G. K. Hall, 1962.
11 vols.
    Begun in 1907, contains references to articles
as well as illustrations which have appeared in 353
magazines of the 19th and 20th centuries, including
many foreign periodicals.   Subject entries only.
Helpful for articles published prior to the beginning
of the Art Index (#44R).   Under subject MUSIC:
Music (by country), Music in Art, Music Halls, etc.,
Carols, Greek Music, Musicians, Opera, Orchestra
and Orchestral Music, Sheet Music Covers, etc.

61(R)   Columbia University.   Libraries.   Avery Architectural
        Library.   Avery Index to Architectural Periodicals.
        2d ed.   Boston: G. K. Hall, 1973.   15 vols.
            Indexed by author and subject, includes all major
        periodicals in the field of architecture published in
        the United States, Great Britain and the British
        Commonwealth, and many other countries (with sum-
        maries in English).   Vol. VIII, subject MUSIC:
        Music Architecture, cross-reference to Architecture
        and Music, Music Halls (see Auditorium, Concert
        Halls, etc.), Musical Instruments, Music of Color,
        Music Rooms, Music Schools.

62   Computer Abstracts.   St. Heller, Jersey, British
        Channel Islands: Technical Information Ltd.,
        1957- .   Supplement: Computer News.
            Title varies: Bibliographical Series, Computers,
        1957-58; Computer Bibliography, 1959; Computer Ab-
        stracts, 1960- .   Indexes over 3,300 abstracts a
        year, in English, of articles and papers in periodi-
        cals, etc.   Covers the world literature on computing
        science.   Subject classification with author index.
        Under subject MUSIC: Music and Computer Compo-
        sition, Computer Music Systems, Electronic Music.

63   Computers and the Humanities.   Vol. 1- .   Flushing,
        New York: Queens College, 1966- .
            Published five times a year with annual biblio-
        graphy which includes the heading MUSIC and articles
        on music and computers, references such as: Music
        Synthesis by Computers.   Music periodicals indexed
        (vol. 4, no. 4, March 1970 checked):   CMS, Council
        for Research in Music Education, FAM, MF, PNM,
        RdM, Sonorum Speculum, etc.

64   Current Index to Journals in Education.   Vol. 1-   .
        New York: Crowell, Collier & Macmillan Informa-
        tion Corp., 1969-   .
            Covers about 20,000 articles in over 700 major
        journals, indexed by ERIC (Educational Resources
        Information Center, U.S. Office of Education).   All
        foreign summaries are translated into English.
        Under MUSIC subject: Music Activities, Music Ap-
        preciation, Music Education, Music Reading, Music
        Techniques, Music Theory, Music Analysis, Musical
        Composition, etc.   Reference is made to the ERIC
        number for the abstract which appears in the main
        entry section of each vol.   Music periodicals in-
        dexed include: JRME, MusEdJ.

65(R)   Dramatic Index.   Boston: Faxon, vols. 1-41, 1909-
        1949.   Cumulated Dramatic Index, 1909-1949.   Bos-
        ton: G. K. Hall, 1963.   2 vols.
            First appeared as Part II of the Annual Magazine
        Subject Index, 1909-1924.   Covers articles and il-
        lustrations concerning the stage and its players in
        the periodicals of America and England.   Under
        subject MUSIC: Folk Music, Bands (Music), Instru-
        mental Music, Jazz, Jewish Music, Moving Pic-
        tures--Music, Music Halls, Musical Festivals, Mu-
        sical Comedies, Musical Instruments, Musicians,
        Opera, Orchestral Music, etc.   Music periodicals
        indexed: Etude, Hollywood Quarterly (now Quarterly
        of Film, Radio and Television), Musician (to 1948).

66(R)   Education Abstracts (UNESCO).   Vols. 1-16, no. 4.
        Paris: United Nations Educational, Scientific and
        Cultural Organization, Education Printing House,
        March 1949-April 1964.
            Vols. 1-3 called: Fundamental Education Ab-
        stracts.   Music periodicals indexed: Etude (to
        1957), Educational Music Magazine, MusEdJ,
        SchMus.

67(R)   Education Index: A Subject Index to the Contents of
        Selected Educational Periodicals.   New York: H.
        W. Wilson, 1929-   .
            Indexes about 200 periodicals, covering all pha-
        ses of education; since 1961 indexes by subject on-
        ly.   Music periodicals indexed: AMT, Educational
        Music Magazine, JRME, MusEdJ, MTNA Proc. (to
        1946), SchMus.

68(R) <u>Engineering Index</u>, 1884- . New York: Engineering
        Magazine, 1892-1919; New York: American Society
        of Mechanical Engineers, 1920- .
        Over 34,000 abstracts or annotations annually of
        articles cited. Indexes current technical periodicals
        selectively. International in scope. Author index.
        Music subject headings as: Acoustics, Electronic
        Music, Computer Sciences, Musical Instruments,
        Sound Recording and Reproduction, etc. No music
        periodicals indexed.

69(R) "Folklore Bibliography," in SFQ, vol. 1- . 1937- .
        First issue of each year, beginning with vol. 2,
        1938, compiled by Ralph S. Biggs. Vol. 25, March
        1961, was compiled by Americo Paredes, with title
        "Folklore Bibliography for 1960." The bibliography
        for 1972 was comp. by Merle E. Simmons. Ameri-
        can material is stressed; relatively strong on Latin
        America. A few annotations are included. Music
        and related periodicals indexed: ETHNO, <u>Folklore</u>
        <u>and Folk Music Archivist</u>, JAF. Special section on
        song, game and dance indexes: JAF, <u>Journal of</u>
        <u>Folklore Institute</u>, <u>Revista Brasileira de Folklore</u>,
        <u>Revista Musical Chilena</u>, SFQ, etc.

70   "Folklore in Periodical Literature," in JAF, vol. 62- .
        1949- .
        Comp. by Richard Dorson to vol. 66, 1953; later
        issues by W. Edson Richmond. Gives partial cov-
        erage to ethnomusicological material, in particular
        to material appearing in folklore journals. Sections:
        Folklore journals, giving title of journal and page
        references to articles in issues of preceding and cur-
        rent year; General publications by author of article.

71   <u>Gravesaner Blätter: Eine Vieteljahresschrift für musi-</u>
        <u>kalische, elektroakustische und schallwissenschaft-</u>
        <u>liche Grenzprobleme (Gravesano Review)</u>. Grave-
        sano, Switzerland: Experimental Studio, 1-Jahrg.
        Nr. 1-29, Juli 1955-1966. Ed. by Hermann Scher-
        chen. Nos. 1-7/8 subtitled in German, nos. 9-29
        in German and English. Suspended during 1963.
        Some nos. accompanied by phonorecords.
        Index to vols. 1-6 in no. 23/24. Articles in Ger-
        man and English, with tendency toward technical and
        scientific subjects. Musically, studies of acoustics,
        tuning, sound properties of concert halls, synthetic

sounds. Subject MUSIC: Music-Acoustics and
Physics, Electro-Acoustics-Periodicals.

72   Guide to Indian Periodical Literature: Social Sciences
      and Humanities. Vol. 1- . Gurgaon: Indian Docu-
      mentation Service, 1964- .
        Subject-author index to articles from about 160
      selected Indian periodicals. Under subject MUSIC:
      Ethnomusicology, Music, Indian, Musical Instru-
      ments, Musicians, Indian. Music and related peri-
      odicals indexed include: Folklore (Calcutta), Jour-
      nal of Music Academy (Madras).

73(R) Historical Abstracts: Bibliography of the World's
        Periodical Literature, 1775-1945. Vol. 1- . Santa
        Barbara, California: American Bibliographic Cen-
        ter, CLIO Press, 1955- .
          Abstracts appearing in 400 periodicals and year-
        books on history of all parts of the world. In Eng-
        lish. Annual author, biographical and subject in-
        dexes. Very little music. Subject MUSIC as: Mu-
        sic, Popular (USA, 1890-1954), Music, History of.
        No music periodicals indexed.

74(R) Index Medicus. Vol. 1- . Washington, D. C.: Nat-
        ional Library of Medicine, 1960- . Cumulated an-
        nually as the Cumulated Index Medicus. Chicago,
        American Medical Association, 1961- .
          Under various titles, this has been published
        regularly since 1879. Author, subject indexes.
        Comprehensive index to the world's medical litera-
        ture, indexing several thousand periodicals, either
        completely or selectively. Subject MUSIC headings
        (Section E): Music in Medicine, Acoustics (Ef-
        fects), Music--Psychology, Music--Therapy, Vocal
        (or) Voice (Medical Effects), Music in Hospitals,
        Occupational Medicine (Music). No music periodi-
        cals indexed, but includes: Journal of the Acousti-
        cal Society of America.

      Index to Art Periodicals see Chicago. Art Insti-
      tute. Ryerson Library.

75   Index to Book Reviews in the Humanities. Vol. 1- .
      Detroit: Phillip Thomson, 1960- .
        Arranged by author of books reviewed. No sub-
      ject or title index. With little duplication of the

Book Review Digest (#51R), indexes book reviews
of several thousand book titles in each issue from
about 675 English-language periodicals. Covers
social sciences as well as the humanities. Reviews
in music periodicals indexed: Canon (Australia),
Canadian Music Journal, ETHNO, JAAC, JAF,
JAMS, JoMT, Listener, M&L, MO, MR, MT, Pan
Pipes, RN, SFQ, etc.

76   Index to Jewish Periodicals: An Author and Subject
Index to Selected American and Anglo-Jewish Journals of General and Scholarly Interest. Vol. 1- .
Cleveland, Ohio: College of Jewish Studies Press,
June 1963- .
Under subject MUSIC: many cross-references
such as Folk Music, Synagogue Music, Israel Composers, Musicians (see also individual names and
subjects), Music, Jewish, Music Conferences (Israel), Music Festivals, Musical Instruments, etc.
No music periodicals found indexed.

77(R) Index to Latin American Periodical Literature, 1929-
1960. Columbus Memorial Library, Pan American
Union (Washington, D. C.); Boston: G. K. Hall,
1962. 8 vols. Suppl. , 1961-1965, 1967.
Periodicals indexed are mostly of Latin American
origin, although many are from the United States
and other parts of the world when articles cited contained information about Latin America or were
written by Latin American authors. The volume
with subject MUSIC is over fifteen pages, three
columns per page. Subject matter is varied, preference given to articles of cultural, economic, educational, historical, legal, political, and social
content. Music periodicals indexed include: Music
Education in the Americas Bul. , Revista Brasileira
de Musica, Revista de Estudios Musicale, and many
other, both music and non-musical, periodical articles.

78   Index to Latin American Periodicals: Humanities and
Social Sciences. Prepared by the Columbus Memorial Library of the Pan American Union. Boston:
G. K. Hall, vols. 1-2, 1961-1962; New York: Scarecrow Press, vols. 3-9, 1963-1969.
Arranged by author, title and subject. With
vol. 3 change of format with subject entries, cross-

references. Author and title index follows. About
250 periodicals indexed with an estimated 50,000
entries; preference given to Spanish periodicals.
Subject under MUSICA: Musica-Argentina, etc.,
Musica Folklorico, etc. Music periodicals indexed
include: Boletin Institute Folklore, Folklore Ameri-
cano (Peru), Revista Musical Chilena.

79(R) Index to Legal Periodicals: An Author and Subject Index to Legal Periodicals and Journals. Vol.1- .
New York: H. W. Wilson, 1909- .
Earlier titles: Index to Legal Periodical Literature, 1888-1924, 1933- . Supplemented 1908- by
the quarterly: Index to Legal Periodicals and Law
Library Journal. Index of selected legal periodicals
published in the United States, Canada, Britain,
Australia and New Zealand. Subject MUSIC: Copyright, Music in the Courts, Music in the Street,
Nuisance of, etc. No music periodicals indexed.

80(R) Index to New Zealand Periodicals. Wellington: National Library of New Zealand, 1940- .
Dictionary index of New Zealand periodicals,
proceedings of certain seminars and conferences
and of articles published elsewhere but pertaining
to New Zealand. Subject index with cross-reference
from author heading. Music periodical indexed
(1973 vol.): New Zealand Listener.

81(R) Index to Periodical Articles By and About Negroes.
Comp. by the Staffs of the Hallie Q. Brown Memorial Library, Central State University, Wilberforce,
Ohio, and the Schomberg Collection of Negro Literature and History, New York Public Library. Boston: G. K. Hall, 1941; 1950- .
Former titles: Index to Selected Periodicals,
1954-1959; Guide to Negro Periodical Literature,
1941; Index to Selected Negro Periodicals, 1950-
1954. Annual, cumulated decennially; arranged by
specific subjects in each of two sections, one rep-
resenting each of the two contributing libraries.
Subject heading MUSIC (1950-1959 cumulation, pp.
325-27): largest number of articles under Musicians
(sub-divided Classical, Popular, Serious); 1960-
1970 cumulation, p. 236, many more music headings. No music periodicals indexed.

82   Index to Religious Periodical Literature: An Author
        and Subject Index to Periodical Literature.
        Vol. 1- . Chicago: American Theological Library
        Association, 1953- .
            Indexes 113 religious and archaeological periodi-
        cals in various languages. Includes an author in-
        dex of book reviews. Policy is not to duplicate the
        indexing in the standard periodical indexes. Sub-
        ject heading MUSIC: Music, Church Music, Hymns,
        Religion and Music, with cross references to other
        pertinent music subjects. No music periodicals in-
        dexed.

83(R)   Index to South Africa Periodicals. Vol. 1- . Johan-
        nesburg: City of Johannesburg Public Library,
        1940- .
            Arranged by author and subject. Music periodi-
        cals indexed (vol. 33, 1973): South Africa Music
        Teacher, African Music. Under subject MUSIC:
        many cross-references.

        Industrial Arts Index   see   Applied Science and
        Technology Index.

84   International Guide to Classical Studies: A Quarterly
        Index to Periodical Literature. Vol. 1- . Darien,
        Conn. : American Bibliographic Service, 1961- .
            Covers the period from the earliest Aegean
        Civilization to the decline of the Roman Empire.
        Two sections: Index to articles and minor works;
        Subject Index. In subject index under MUSIC: Mu-
        sic, Musical Instruments, Music, Late Greek, etc.
        with references to item numbers in the volume.
        No music periodicals indexed.

85   International Guide to Medieval Studies: A Quarterly
        Index to Periodical Literature. Vol. 1- . Darien,
        Conn. : American Bibliographic Service, June
        1961- .
            Covers periodical literature pertaining roughly to
        the sixth through the fourteenth centuries. Text in
        English and European languages. Frequent descrip-
        tive annotations. Under subject heading MUSIC:
        cross-references to Trouveres, Walter von der Vo-
        gelweide, etc. Related to music periodical indexed:
        Spec.

International Index to Periodicals   see   Social
Sciences and Humanities Index.

86   International Medieval Bibliography.   Minneapolis:
      Leeds, 1968.   2 vols.
         Bibliography of articles and books, arranged by
      author and subject.   About 1,500 items, with 148
      serials indexed.   Music and related periodicals in-
      dexed: AfMW, AM, Folklore (London), GSJ, JAMS,
      MD, MQ, M&L, MR, PMA, RdM, RenN, Spec.,
      Archiv für Liturgiewissenschaft.

87(R) Internationale Bibliographie der Rezensionen wissen-
       schaftlicher Literatur.   Hrsg. von Otto Zeller.
       Abteilung C: Internationale Bibliographie der Zeit-
       schriften-Literatur.   Osnabrück: Felix Dietrich,
       1897-1944.
          International bibliography of book reviews of
       scholarly literature.   Listed under author, review-
       er.   Book reviews in non-German periodicals have
       been added, listed in a separate section.   Music
       reviews in music periodicals in: M&L, MF, MQ,
       MR, MusEdJ, Musica, etc.

88(R) Jackson, Bruce, comp.   The Negro and His Folklore
       in 19th-Century Periodicals.   Ed., with an intro-
       duction, by Bruce Jackson.   (Bibliographical and
       Special Series of the American Folklore Society,
       18.) Austin, Texas: University of Texas Press,
       1967.   394p.
          Chronologically arranged, 1838-1899.   Anthology
       of thirty-three articles and reviews from 19th-cen-
       tury American periodicals on Negro folksong,
       speech, belief, custom, story (non-musical folk-
       lore), a few stage minstrelsy showing contemporary
       attitudes.   Periodicals are mostly well-known, pop-
       ular literary types, with one musical periodical in-
       cluded: Dwight's Journal of Music (four articles).
       Appendix II/B: list of articles in JAF, 1888-1901;
       II/C: articles in Southern Workman, 1893-1901;
       II/D: some other articles on Negro folklore in
       19th-century periodicals.

89(R) Journal of Aesthetics and Art Criticism: An Index of
       Articles and Book Reviews Pertaining to Music,
       Including a Selection of Articles on Related Sub-
       jects, 1941-1964.   Comp. by Peter Louis Ciurzak.

Emporia, Kansas: Kansas State Teachers' College,
January 31, 1965. 15p. Typescript.
JAAC, vol.1/1, Spring 1941--vol.22/4, Summer
1964; quarterly devoted to the advancement of aesthetics and the arts. "Aesthetics includes all the
studies of the arts and related types of experience
from a philosophic, scientific, or other theoretical
standpoint.... " In two sections: author list of articles with complete citations, with a few short annotations; reviews, and reviewers. To be published
in the Music Library Association Index Series.

90(R) Journal of American Folk-Lore. Index, vols.1-40,
1888-1927, issued as vol.14 of the Memoirs of the
American Folk-Lore Society. Comp. by Tristam
P. Coffin: An Analytical Index to the JAF, vols.
1-70, 1888-1957. (Bibliographical and Special
Series, 7) Philadelphia: American Folklore Society,
1958. NOTE: List of articles in JAF, 1888-1901,
in Jackson (# 88R)
Source material for all regions in the United
States: ballads, songs, games, customs, etc.,
from the entire country, much of which is not
available elsewhere. Review of Coffin Index by
Evelyn K. Wells, in JIFMC, vol.11, 1959, p.108:
classifies 1) titles of articles, 2) authors of articles, 3) book reviews, 4) news and notices, 5) subjects and areas in folklore (fifty-nine sub-divisions),
5) nationalities and ethnic groups, 7) titles and
first significant lines of songs and rimes (60 pages),
8) tales.

91   Kirkland, Edward Capers. Bibliography of South Asian
Folklore (Folklore Institute Monography Series,
vol.21) Bloomington, Indiana: Indiana University,
1966. 291p.
From review by Alton C. Morris in SFQ,
vol.30/4, 1966, pp.345-7: "has almost 7,000 entries from publications in many languages, and from
various Indian regional languages and dialects ...
with subjects such as superstition, proverbs, folk-
tales, folksongs, legends, etc. Index listings by
folklore genres, linguistic groups, etc. References
from periodicals: 168 of all types covering areas
widely dispersed as Bombay, London, Copenhagen
and Berkeley, California. "

92   Library and Information Science Abstracts. Vol. 1- .
      London: Library Association, January/February
      1969- .
          Supersedes Library Science Abstracts, vols. 1-
      19/4, January/May 1950-December 1968. Classi-
      fied subject index arranged with annual author and
      subject indexes. International, with titles/abstracts
      in English. Subject heading MUSIC: Music Libra-
      ries, Music Departments, Music Library Materials,
      Music: Subject Bibliographies. Music periodical
      indexed/abstracted: NOTES.

93   Library Literature: An Index to Library and Informa-
      tion Science. New York: H. W. Wilson, 1933- .
          Author and subject index to materials on library
      and information science, to books, pamphlets and
      periodical literature relating to libraries and libra-
      rianship. Subject headings under MUSIC include:
      Music in the Library, Music Libraries and Collec-
      tions. Music periodicals indexed: FAM (since
      1972), NOTES.

      Magazine Subject Index see Cumulated Magazine
      Subject Index.

94   Mental Health Book Review Index: An Annual Biblio-
      graphy of Books and Book Reviews in the Behavioral
      Sciences. New York: New York University, 1956-
      1972, nos. 1-22.
          Cumulative author-title index, vols. 1-2, 1956-
      1967. Issued as a suppl. to the Psychological
      Newsletter, January 1956-1972. Arranged by name
      of author of book reviewed. Each annual issue lists
      about 300 books, selected and reviewed by special-
      ists, based on book reviews appearing in 220 jour-
      nals in the English language, each with references
      to three or more reviews. Coverage: psychology,
      psychiatry, psychoanalysis. Music periodical in-
      dexed: Journal of Music Therapy.

95   New Hungarian Quarterly. Vol. 1- . Budapest: Cor-
      vina Press, 1960- .
          Continuation of Hungarian Quarterly, 1936-1942.
      Section in each issue on "Music Life"--new record-
      ings, new publications. Articles and issues es-
      pecially on and by Hungarian authors and composers
      as: Bartók, Kodály.

96   Philosophers' Index: An International Index to Philo-
        sophical Periodicals. Bowling Green, Ohio: Bowl-
        ing Green University, Spring 1967- .
            Subject and author index to all major American
        and British philosophical periodicals, selected jour-
        nals in other languages and related interdisciplinary
        publications. Subject headings for MUSIC: Music,
        Musical, Musicals, Musicology. Music-related
        periodicals indexed: British Journal of Aesthetics,
        JAAC.

97(R)   Psychological Abstracts. Lancaster, Pennsylvania:
        American Psychological Association, 1927- .
        Cumulated Subject Index, 1927-1960. Boston: G.
        K. Hall, 1966. 2 vols. Supplements, 1961-1968.
        2 vols. Author Index, 1927-1958. Boston: G. K.
        Hall, 1960. 5 vols.
            Continuation of Psychological Index (#98R).
        Lists new books and articles on psychology and re-
        lated subjects with signed abstract of each item.
        Author index to each number and full author and
        subjects to each vol. Over 500 serial publications
        of the world are abstracted. Titles are given in the
        original language and in English translation; ab-
        stracts are in English. Subject headings under MU-
        SIC (June 1974): Music, Music Education, Music
        Therapy, Musical Ability, Musical Instruments, etc.
        Music periodicals indexed: Etude (to 1957), Jour-
        nal of Music Therapy, JRME, MQ, MusEdJ, MusJ;
        related: JAAC.

98(R)   Psychological Index, 1894-1935. Princeton, New Jer-
        sey: Psychological Review Co. , 1895-1936. 42
        vols. Author Index, 1894-1935. Boston: G. K.
        Hall, 1960. 5 vols.
            Books and articles in many languages are classi-
        fied, arranged with an author index, but no subject
        index. Indexes about 350 periodicals. Continued
        by Psychological Abstracts (#97R).

99   Religious and Theological Abstracts. Vol. 1- . My-
        erstown, Pennsylvania: Religious and Theological
        Abstracts, Inc. , March 1958- .
            Abstracts of articles from a selection of Chris-
        tian, Jewish, Moslem journals, in various languages.
        Author and subject index. Subject headings under
        MUSIC as: Hymnody, Liturgy, Music and Hymnody,
        Music, etc. No music periodicals indexed.

100   Research in Education: A Monthly Abstract Journal
        (ERIC).   Washington, D. C. :   U. S. Office of Edu-
        cation, 1966- .
        Annual subject, author, institution index issued
        by the Educational Resources Information Center.
        Subject headings for MUSIC: Music Appreciation--
        Education, --Teachers, --Theory, etc. Musical
        Composition, Musical Instruments, Music Theory,
        Music Activities, etc.

101(R) Salem, James M.   Guide to Critical Reviews.   Four
        Parts. 2d ed.   New York: Scarecrow Press,
        1976.   Part II: The Musical, 1909-1974.   619p.
        Reviews of musicals on the New York stage
        with title, book, music, lyrics, staging, opening
        date, American and Canadian periodicals and the
        New York Times reviews. Various indexes:
        authors, composers, lyricists, directors, design-
        ers, choreographers, original writers and authors,
        titles.

102   Science Abstracts.   Section C: Computer and Control
        Abstracts.   London: Institute of Electrical Engi-
        neers, 1969- .
        Under subject heading HUMANITIES: Music,
        Computer Application, Music, Computer Composi-
        tion, Musical Acoustics, Music, Electronic, Mu-
        sic Theory (CAI Program comparisons), etc.

103(R) "Selective Current Bibliography for Aesthetics and
        Related Fields, " JAAC, vol. 1- . 1941- .
        Appears in the last issue of each vol. , comp.
        by Helmut Hungerland, current editor, Elmer H.
        Duncan.   Publications considered important "for
        the philosophical, scientific, or other theoretical
        study of the arts and related phenomena. " Vol.
        31/4, 1974, pp. 573-90, bibliography for Janu-
        ary--December 1972, has divisions: Aesthetics
        as the philosophy of art; Aesthetics as the psy-
        chology of art; Historical studies; Testing, experi-
        ments and therapy; Aesthetic education.   Articles
        on music and musicology are scattered throughout
        the bibliography.   Music periodicals indexed:
        AM, DM, HF, ETHNO, JAMS, JMT,
        JRME, M&L, MO, MQ, MR, MT, PNA, RaM,
        Score.

104(R)   Social Sciences and Humanities Index.   Vol. 1- .
         New York: H. W. Wilson, 1907- .
         Title varies: Readers' Guide to Periodical
         Literature, Suppl., 1907-1919; International Index,
         1920-March 1965. Since April 1965 limited to
         periodicals in the social sciences and humanities,
         most of which are published in the United States.
         Stresses learned journals, those not included in
         the Readers' Guide ... (#38R). Author-subject
         index. Under subject MUSIC, 1967/1968 vol.:
         about two columns. Music periodicals indexed
         (vol. 1): JAF, SFQ; vol. 12: M&L, MR, NOTES;
         vol. 13: added MQ; vol. 15, 1958/1960: all noted
         so far, etc.

105   Sociological Abstracts. Vol. 1- . New York: So-
         ciological Abstracts, Inc., January 1953- .
         Abstracts of periodical articles, monographs
         and books, internationally. Classified subject ar-
         rangement, with author index. Indexes about 500
         journals on sociology selectively. Annual cumula-
         tive index. On subject MUSIC as: Music, Im-
         pact of Primitive on Occidental, Musicians, Dance,
         Profession. No music periodicals indexed.

106(R)   South, Earl Bennett. Index of Periodical Literature
         on Testing, 1921-1936. New York: The Psycho-
         logical Corp., 1937. 282p.
         Arranged by author, numbered serially, 1-255,
         with 5,005 items listed. Subject index, pp. 256-
         82, includes many references under MUSIC as:
         Ability, Achievement, Guidance in, Mental Age
         and Prognosis in, Psychological, Study of, Survey
         of, Testing, etc. Music periodicals indexed in-
         clude: MENC Proc., MusEdJ, Musician, Music
         Supervisors' National Conference, National Acade-
         my of Music Training--Proceedings.

         Subject Index to Periodicals see British Humani-
         ties Index.

107(R)   Writers' Program, New York. The Film Index: A
         Bibliography. Vol. 1- . New York: Museum of
         Modern Art Film Library and H. W. Wilson,
         1941- .
         Vol. 1, 1941: The Film as Art: Music, pp. 202-
         11, in two divisions: Silent era, pp. 202-07, Sound

era, pp. 207-11.   Music periodicals indexed:
Etude (to 1957), M&L, MM, MQ, MT, Metronome,
Musician, and related periodicals.

108   Yearbook of Liturgical Studies.   Vol. 1- .   Indiana:
Notre Dame University, 1960- .
Bibliography, each year, of articles recently
published, principally in Europe and North America, concerning the historical development of the
liturgy and current liturgical practices.   Classified
by topic.   Frequent descriptive annotations.   Auth-
or and subject index.   Vol. 4, 1963, "Survey of
Liturgical Literature" MUSIC, items 654-94, indexes: Études Grégoriennes, Liturgical Arts,
Liturgisches Jahrbuch, MQ, Musica Sacra.

Part V

MUSIC PERIODICAL LITERATURE IN
MUSIC INDEXES AND BIBLIOGRAPHIES

109(R) Aber, Adolf. Handbuch der Musikliteratur in system-
        atisch-chronologischer Anordung. (Kleine Hand-
        bücher der Musikgeschichte nach Gattungen, 13)
        Leipzig: Breitkopf & Härtel, 1922. Reprint:
        Hildesheim: Olm, 1967. 696 cols.
        Indexes 133 music periodicals and other serial
        publications. Covers the period from about 1700-
        1922. Under subject with author and name in-
        dexes. International, but strong in German mat-
        erials. Music periodicals indexed include: AfMW,
        AMZ, Bach-Jahrbuch, Bayreuther Blätter, Caeci-
        lia (1874-1964), MMR (1871-1960), MA, MT,
        MusAmer, RM, RMI.

110(R) Abravanel, Claude. Claude Debussy: A Bibliography.
        (Detroit Studies in Music Bibliography, 29) De-
        troit: Information Coordinators, Inc. , 1974.
        214p.
        List of 1, 854 items with divisions: Bibliograph-
        ical Works, Books on Debussy, General (Chapters
        in books, encyclopedias, general literature), Peri-
        odicals (including special numbers as RM), Bio-
        graphical articles, Literature on the relations of
        Debussy, Technique and style, Music Works, Per-
        sonal Non-Musical Activities, Critical and Litera-
        ry Works, Indexes by author, reviewer; list of
        periodicals analyzed, by country, Argentina--Yugo-
        slavia, with references by item number to article
        or review in the text.

111(R) Acta Musicologica. Index, vols. 1-25, 1928-1953, in
        vol. 25, fasc. 4, pp. 180-89. Vols. 26-39 include
        an index of names cited in each vol. (prepared
        for the last eleven vols. by Theodore Holm.)
        Kassel: International Musicological Society,
        1928- .

112(R) _____. Index, vols. 1-39, Fall 1928-Spring 1967.
        Comp. by Cecil Adkins and Alis Dickinson. Basel:
        Bärenreiter, n. d.
            Arranged in two parts: Author index, lists ar-
        ticles chronologically in order of publication;
        classified subject index. Appendix: Society News,
        Questions, Notices, Bibliographies of New Books
        Indexed.

113(R) Allgemeine musikalische Zeitung. Vols. 1-50. Leip-
        zig: Breitkopf & Härtel, October 1798-December
        1848.
            Quoted from article by J. Murray Barbour,
        "AMZ, Prototype of Contemporary Musical Journa-
        lism," NOTES, 5/3, (June 1948), 325-37: "Musi-
        cal supplements appeared regularly for the first
        twenty-five years, then less often, and not at all
        for the last ten or twelve years." Composers
        represented: Haydn, Beethoven, Mozart, Cheru-
        bini, Palestrina, Reichardt, Zumsteeg.

114   Aning, B. A. An Annotated Bibliography of Music
        and Dance in English-Speaking Africa. Legon:
        Institute of African Studies, University of Ghana,
        1967, 47p.
            From the review by Alan P. Merriam in ETH-
        NO, 16/3, September 1972, 544-5: All entries
        are of books and articles (132 items) written in
        English. Annotated bibliography of sources deal-
        ing with music and dance, music in dance, or
        dance in music. Organized by countries and
        grouped under geographic regions. Index of
        authors.

115   Annotated Guide to Periodical Literature on Church
        Music, 1972: A Comprehensive Reference Guide
        to Significant Signed Feature Articles on Church
        Music Appearing in American Music Periodicals
        in 1972. Prepared by the editors of Music Ar-
        ticle Guide (#229), Philadelphia, Pennsylvania:
        1973. 40p.
            Articles extracted from issues of Music Ar-
        ticle Guide, first published in 1972 for the year
        1971. Sections: Bells and Bell Programs,
        Choirs and Choral Art, Church Music, Hymnology,
        Organ, Sacred Music. Music periodicals indexed:
        American Choral Review, AMT, Church Music,

CJ, Clavier, Diapason, Hymn, Journal of Church
Music, Musart (Washington, D. C.), Music Minis-
try, Music: AGO-RCCO Magazine, MusEdJ, MQ,
NATS Bul., etc.

116   Annual Bibliography of European Ethnomusicology.
Vol. 1- . Hrsg. von Slowakischen National-Mu-
seum in Vergindung mit dem Institut für Musik-
wissenschaften und dem Institut für Berlin, unter
Mitwirkung des International Folk Music Council.
Bratislava: 1967- .
Bibliography covers only ethnomusicological
publications published in Europe, dealing with folk
music, "primitive" and oriental music, as well as
those concerned with dance forms, publications of
scientific character, as source-collections of
songs, music, dance, catalogues of musical instruments, lists of sources and bibliographies, books,
papers, articles, etc. Entries are printed in the
original language with an English, German or
French translation. Indexes: Authors, Geograph-
ical-Ethnical Survey, Fields of Research. Rela-
ted-to-music periodicals indexed: Folk Music Journal, Folklore (London), IFMC Yearbook, Proceedings of the Scottish Anthropological and Folklore
Society.

117(R) Apel, Willi. Harvard Dictionary of Music. 2d ed.,
rev. & enl. Cambridge, Massachusetts: The
Belknap Press of Harvard University, 1969.
935p.
Indexes over forty periodicals and other serial
publications in various languages, mostly from the
beginning of the 20th century, to current articles.
Under subject, bibliographic entries list important,
essential articles.

118   Armitage, Andrew D. and Tudor, Dean, comp. Annual Index to Popular Music Record Reviews.
Metuchen, New Jersey: Scarecrow Press, 1972-
Reviews of long-playing recordings of popular
music appearing in about sixty periodicals. Under twelve categories: Rock, Mood-Pop, Country,
Folk, Ethnic, Jazz, Blues, Rhythm and Blues &
Soul, Religious Music, Stage & Show, Band, Hu-
mor. Includes a scalar evaluation of approval or
disapproval. Indexes: Artist, Anthology, Con-

certs. Music periodicals indexed include: ARG,
Audio, Downbeat, English Dance & Song, ETHNO,
Gramophone, HF, JAF, MusJ, and many others.

119(R) Arnold, Corliss Richard. Organ Literature: A
Comprehensive Survey. Metuchen, New Jersey:
Scarecrow Press, 1973. 673p.
Part I: Historical survey, 1300-1970: earliest
published and manuscript organ music in Western
Europe; Part II: Biographical section. Appendix:
Organ works of J. S. Bach. Bibliography,
pp. 615-34, indexes articles in music periodicals,
including: American Guild of Organists, American
Organists, Diapason, JAMS, MO, M&L, MQ, MR,
MT, MD, PMA, Music/AGO-RCCO Magazine, RM,
Spec., etc.

120   "Articles Concerning Music in Non-Musical Journals,
1949-1964. " CM, Spring 1965, pp. 121-27; Fall
1965, pp. 221-26; Spring 1966, pp. 97-103.
Source of list, Social Sciences and Humanities
Index (#104R) and its predecessor, International
Index of Periodicals. First installment, articles
considered in an historical context; 2d installment,
articles on philosophy, literature, psychology,
acoustics; 3d installment, folk music, non-western
music, Americana. The last installment noted the
name of the compiler, Susan Thiemann.

121(R) Austin, William W. Music in the Twentieth Century
from Debussy Through Stravinsky. New York:
W. W. Norton, 1966. 708p.
Copious annotated bibliography, pp. 552-662.
Divisions: International and Regional; Surveys:
National; Composers and Other Musicians; Jazz
(excluding items devoted to a single individual);
Experimental Music (microtones, electronic music,
musique concrète, etc.); Bibliographies; Miscel-
laneous. Music periodicals indexed: ACA Bul.,
AfMW, Canadian Music Journal, JAMS, JoMT, MF,
M&L, MMR, MQ, MR, MT, NOTES, NZfM,
PNM, RM, SMZ, ZfMW.

122(R) Bahler, Peter Benjamin. Electronic and Computer
Music: An Annotated Bibliography of Writings in
English. Thesis, M. A., Department of Theory,
Eastman School of Music, University of Rochester,

1966.   130p.
Articles published before 1966, with a brief
description of each work.   Chapter I: Electronic
music, concrete music, tape record music, with
205 annotated entries and twelve not annotated.
Chapter II; Computer music, with sixty-three an-
notated entries, fourteen not.   Music and related
periodicals indexed: ACA Bul., AMT, ARG,
Etude (to 1957), Film Music, HF, Gravesaner
Blätter, Instrum, JoMT, Journal of the Audio
Engineering Society, MT, MusJ, MQ, PNA, Die
Reihe, MO, MR, Score, Downbeat, Journal of the
Acoustical Society, etc.

123(R) Baker, Theodore.   Baker's Biographical Dictionary
of Musicians.   5th ed., rev. by Nicolas Slonim-
sky.   New York: G. Schirmer, 1958.   1,855p.
Supplements, 1965, 1971.   143p. and 262p.
No separate list of periodical articles in respective bibliographies.   Many from music periodicals as well as non-music periodicals.

124(R) Basart, Ann Phillips.   Bibliography of Writings on
Twentieth-Century Music.   In progress.
Approximately 80,000 entries announced in 1974.
Annotated.   Classified arrangement.   Author and
subject indexes.   To be published.   Source:
Checklist of Music Bibliographies and Indexes in
Progress and Unpublished.   3d ed.   (M. L. A.
Series Index Series, 3).   1974

125(R) _____.   Serial Music: A Classified Bibliography
of Writings on Twelve-Tone and Electronic Music.
(University of California Bibliographic Guides)
Berkeley: University of California Press, 1961.
151p.
Division into four sections: Twelve-tone music;
Electronic Music; Viennese School (Schoenberg,
Berg, Webern); Other composers who use serial
techniques (arranged alphabetically by composer).
Short, descriptive annotations.   Music periodicals
indexed: AMS Bul., AMS Papers, JAMS, M&L,
MMR, MQ, MR, Music Survey, NOTES, NZFM,
RM, RMI, RaM, PMA, SMZ, Score, ZfMW.

126(R) Belknap, Sara Yancy.   Guide to Dance Periodicals:
An Analytical Index of Articles.   Vols.1-7, 1931-

1956, various places, publishers, dates; Vols. 8-10.
Metuchen, New Jersey: Scarecrow Press, 1960-
1963. From 1966, incorporated in Guide to the
Performing Arts (#128).
   Subject and selective author index. Nineteen
periodicals indexed, English and American.

127   . Guide to the Musical Arts: An Analytical
Index of Articles and Illustrations, 1953-1956.
Metuchen, New Jersey: 1957-1959. Superseded
by Guide to the Performing Arts (#128).
   While a considerable amount of material dupli-
cates listings in the Music Index (#231), some
15,000 articles are indexed dealing with music,
opera, the dance and the theater. In general,
includes those periodicals published from 1953-
1956, in a few cases back to 1949. Music periodicals indexed include: Canadian Music Journal,
International Musician, Juilliard Review, MusCour,
OpN, MQ, etc.

128   . Guide to the Performing Arts. Vols. 1-12.
1957-1968. Metuchen, New Jersey: Scarecrow
Press, 1960-1972. From 1968, new compilers:
Louis Rachow and Katherine Hartley.
   Annual index to selected periodicals in the performing arts. References to performing groups
as well as general subject headings. In 1968 for-
ty-eight publications are indexed on theater and
drama, dance, music, opera, cinema, radio and
TV, etc. Limited to United States and Canada.
Music periodical indexed: NOTES.

129   . "Latin-American Performing Arts: An
Analytical Index: 1957-1958." Inter-American
Music Bul., no.17, May 1960, 1-110.
   Subject-author index. Music periodicals in-
dexed: Americas, Boletín Inter-Americano de
Música, Buenos Aires Musical, Centro--Americana
(1957), Inter-American Music Bul., Pro Arte Mu-
sical (Havana), Revista Musical Chilena.

130   Berlind, Gary, et al., comp. "Writings on the Use
of Computers in Music." CMS, 6, (Fall 1966),
143-57.
   Music and related periodicals indexed: Arts
and Architecture, FAM, Gravesaner Blätter,
ETHNO, JAAC, JAF, JoMT, Melos, MusAmer,
RM, M&L.

Part V   39

131(R) "Bibliographie der Aufsätze zur Musik in aussermusi-
        kalischen italienischen Zeitschriften. " Analecta
        Musicologia, Veröffentlichungen der Musikabteilung
        des deutschen historischen Instituts in Rom. Bd.
        1, (1963), 90-112; Bd. 2, (1965), 114-228)
        Bibliography of writings on music in Italian
        non-musical journals. Part I comp. by Paul
        Kast; Part 2 by Ernst Ludwig Berg. The two
        installments are organized and indexed independent-
        ly; the first part has 237 items listed with six
        Italian non-musical periodicals checked; the second
        part has 1, 074 items listed with fifteen Italian non-
        musical periodicals indexed. Both have author and
        subject indexes.

132(R) Bibliographie des Musikschrifttums. Leipzig; Frank-
        furt a. Main: F. Hofmeister, 1936- . Editors,
        1936-37: Kurt Taut; 1938-39: Georg Karstädt;
        1940-1949, publication suspended; 1950- , ed. by
        Wolfgang Schmieder.
             Continuation of the book lists in JMP (1895-
        1941) Bibliography of books and an index to peri-
        odical literature in all European languages. Se-
        lection of articles have tendency toward scholarly
        and original contributions. Many non-musical
        journals included. Indexes: Subjects, Places,
        Names as Subjects, Authors. Music periodicals
        indexed include: African Music, AM, AfMW,
        ETHNO, FAM, MF, MQ, NZfM, NOTES, PMA,
        etc.

133   "Bibliography of Current Periodical Literature. "
        JoMT, 1/1, March 1957- .
             Vols. 1-3 comp. by Donald Loach, George H.
        Jacobson; vol. 4/1, April 1960, not signed; from
        vol. 5, title changed to "Recent Books and Arti-
        cles. " Under subject of music theory, music and
        related periodicals indexed: AfMW, AM, Canadian
        Music Journal, Gregorian Review, JAAC, JAMS,
        JRME, JoMT, M&L, MF, MQ, MR, MT, MMR,
        etc.

134(R) A Bibliography of Periodical Literature in Musicology
        and Allied Fields. No. 1, October 1, 1938-Sep-
        tember 30, 1939; No. 2, October 1, 1939-September
        30, 1940. Washington, D. C. : American Council
        of Learned Societies, 1940-1943. 2 vols.
             Vol. 1 comp. by D. H. Daugherty; vol. 2

added Leonard Ellinwood and Richard S. Hill.
About 300 music and non-musical periodicals
were examined, 148 of which were found to
contain relevant articles.   These represent:
literature, history, anthropology, archaeology,
physics, psychology and other fields besides
music.   Many of the articles have signed
abstracts or annotations. Sixty-eight music
periodicals were indexed.

135(R)   Blom, Eric.   A General Index to Modern Musical
Literature in the English Language, Including
Periodicals for the Years, 1915-1925. London:
J. Curwen, 1927. 159p.
Author and subject index with references to
sections of a book listed.   No annotations.   Amer-
ican publications not represented, unless of "first
importance."   Music periodicals indexed: British
Musician, Chesterian, M&L, MO, MT, PMA,
Sackbut, and the American music periodical, MQ.

136(R)   Blum, Fred.   Jean Sibelius, an International Bibliography on the Occasion of the Centennial Celebra-
tions, 1965.   (Detroit Studies in Music Bibliography, 8) Detroit: Information Coordinators,
1965. 114p.
Music periodicals indexed from the United
States, England, Germany, Australia, Switzerland,
pp. 47-71; non-musical journals, pp. 73-94. Many
are annotated, descriptively and/or critically.

137(R)   Bobillier, Marie [Michel Brenet, Pseud.] "Biblio-
graphie des Bibliographies Musicale." L'Année
Musicale, 3, (1913), 1-152.
Lists general works and periodical articles by
author.   Music periodicals indexed include: AMZ,
Kirchenmusikalisches Jahrbuch, MfMG, RMI,
SIM, VfMW.

138   Bowen, Jean and Jackson, Paul T. "A Study of
Periodicals Indexed in NOTES' Index to Record
Reviews." NOTES, 22/2, (Winter 1965/1966)
945-55.
Fall 1964 issue of NOTES lists twenty-eight
periodicals indexed for record reviews. All but
four of these are considered for this survey.
All are in English.   Periodicals are grouped

here by subject or field of interest: General
literary and political magazines; Consumer service magazines; Library Journal (in a class by it-
self); Folklore magazines; General music magazines; Scholarly music magazines; Record magazines.

139(R) Brass Quarterly. Ed. by Mary Rasmussen. Mil-
ford, New Hampshire: The Cabinet Press.
vol. 1/1-vol. 7/4, 1957-1964. Continued as Brass
and Woodwind Quarterly, vol. 1/1/2-vol. 2/1/2,
1966-1969.
Bibliographic series in successive issues of
this periodical. Each installment covers books
and articles published during a five-year period
on wind music, etc. Music periodicals indexed
include: Etude (to May/June 1957), Instrum,
Journal of the Acoustical Society of America,
Metronome, NZfM, RM, SchMus, ZfMW, etc.

Brenet, Michel, pseud. see Bobillier, Marie.

140(R) British Museum (London) Department of Printed
Books. Catalogue of Printed Music Published Between 1487 and 1800 Now in the British Museum.
Ed. by W. Barclay Squire. London: The Trustees, 1912. 2 vols. Reprint by Kraus, 1969.
First Suppl. (bound in), 134p. Second Suppl., ed.
by W. C. Smith, Cambridge University Press,
1940. 85p.
Under heading "Periodical Publications," considerable number of entries for musical works
published in British and foreign periodicals.
Brief entries with some dates of publication.

141(R) _____. Hand-List of Music Published in Some
British and Foreign Periodicals Between 1787
and 1848, Now in the British Museum. London:
The Trustees, 1962. 80p.
Index to music (mostly songs) in twelve periodicals: 1,855 entries arranged by composer. Music periodicals indexed include: AMZ (1798-1848),
La Belle Assemblée (London, 1806-1807), Caecilia
(1824-1848), The Harmonicon (London, 1823-1833),
etc.

142(R) Brook, Barry S. Thematic Catalogues in Music: An
Annotated Bibliography. Hillsdale, New York:

Pendragon Press, 1972.   347p.
Published under the joint sponsorship of the
Music Library Association and RILM Abstracts.
Over forty music periodicals have been checked.

143(R)   Bukofzer, Manfred F.   Music in the Baroque Era,
from Monteverdi to Bach.   New York, W. W.
Norton, 1947.   489p.
Bibliography, pp. 433-449, includes many periodical articles concerning the Baroque era.   List
is by author.   Music periodicals indexed include:
MM, MQ, PMA, RM, RMI, SIM, etc.

144(R)   Carl Gregor, Duke of Mecklenburg.   Bibliographie
einiger Grenzgebiete der Musikwissenschaft.
(Bibliographica Aureliana, 6) Baden-Baden: Li-
brairie Heizt, 1962.   200p.
Bibliography of books and periodical articles on
areas bordering on historial musicology.   Includes
such subjects as: aesthetics, psychology, sociology of music, music and other arts, musical inter-
ests of poets, writers, etc.   3,519 entries, with
indexes: Persons, Subjects.

145   Carlson, Effie B.   A Bio-Bibliographical Dictionary
of Twelve-Tone and Serial Composers.   Metuchen,
New Jersey: Scarecrow Press, 1970.   233p.
"History of twentieth-century piano music as a
framework for understanding the role of serial
composition in contemporary music. "   Part 1,
lists piano works of Berg, Schoenberg, and Webern.
Part 2 has about eighty entries of a representative
group of composers who have written twelve-tone,
serial, or serially-oriented piano music from Gilbert Amy to Bernd Alois Zimmerman.   Music
periodicals indexed: HF, JoMT, Melos, MQ,
MusAmer, PNM, Die Reihe, RN, Score, etc.

146(R)   Cavanagh, Beverley.   "Annotated Bibliography of Es-
kimo Music. "   ETHNO, 16, (1972), 479-87.
Music and musical traditions of the Eskimos of
Greenland, the Canadian Arctic, and Alaska.   Mu-
sic and related periodicals indexed: American
Anthropologist, JAF, MQ, MusEdJ, MusAmer,
SMZ.

147(R)   Chase, Gilbert, comp.   Bibliography of Latin American Folk Music.   Washington, D. C. :   Library of

Congress, Music Division, 1942. Reprint, AMS
Press, 1972. Mimeograph. 141p. and several
unnumbered pages.
1,122 items listed which include many music
periodical articles on the subject of Latin American folk music.

148(R) The Chesterian. Index, vols.1-10, September 1919-
July 1929. London, Novello, 1930.
Indexed by 1) author, 2) subject.

149 College Music Symposium. Index to Proceedings and
Symposium, vols.1-12, 1958-1972. Comp. by
Craig Short. CMS, 12, (Fall 1972), 197-215.
Indexed by 1) author, 2) reviews, 3) subjects.

150 Composer (London). Index, 1962-1972; no.48, Sum-
mer 1973. Comp. by Robert Baker. London:
Composers' Guild of Great Britain.
Indexed by author, subject and title.

151 Consumers Union Reviews Classical Recordings, by
CU's Music Consultant and the Editors of Consumers Reports. New York, Indianapolis: Bobbs-
Merrill, 1973. 376p.
Alphabetically arranged by composer, gives pertinent information, including price, and date of
pressing for each selection. Separate indexes:
Orchestras and Groups; Conductors; Performers;
Composers. Review of each recording with added
comment as to other recordings of same composer
and title.

152 Coover, James, comp. "Music Theory in Translation: A Bibliography." JoMT, 3/1, (April 1959),
70-96. Suppl., 1959-1969, 13/2 (1969), 230-248.
English translations of early music theoretical
works. Music periodicals indexed: JoMT, MD,
MQ.

153 Cross, Lowell M., comp. Bibliography of Electronic
Music. Canada: University of Toronto, 1967.
126p.
1,563 articles listed from the 1950's and 1960's.
No annotations. Indexes: Author, with some subject matter. Music periodicals indexed include:
Canadian Music Journal, CM, ACA Bul., DM,

JAAC, JIFMC, JoMT, Melos, MO, MT, PMA,
NZfM, MQ, RbM, and many others.

154   Crow, Todd, comp., ed. Bartók Studies. (Detroit
         Reprints in Music) Detroit: Information Coordina-
         tors, 1976. 300p.
              Selective bibliography, pp. 216-289, of twenty-
         seven significant books and articles written on
         Bartók during the period 1963-1973, all of which
         appeared in The New Hungarian Quarterly. Li-
         bretti of two of Bartók's stage works included,
         also a sheaf of letters.

155   "Current Bibliography in Ethnomusicology. " ETHNO,
         vol. 1- . Middletown, Conn. : Wesleyan Univer-
         sity, Journal of the Society for Ethnomusicology,
         December 1953- .
              Predecessor: Ethnomusicology Newsletter,
         no. 1, 1951- . Nearly every issue includes a
         "Current Bibliography" of books and articles in
         the field of ethnomusicology. By various com-
         pilers, organized by geographical areas and topics.
         The December 1953 issue, comp. by Mary Ann
         Rediske, was on Africa; in September 1972, comp.
         by Joseph C. Hickerson, Neil V. Rosenberg and
         Frank J. Gillis, it was called "Current Biblio-
         graphy and Discography. "

156   Current Musicology. Index, nos. 1-10, 1965-1970.
              Comp. by Thomas W. Baker, CM, no. 11, 1971,
         134-149.

157(R)   Davidsson, Åke. Bibliographie zur Geschichte des
         Musikdrucks. (Studia Musicologica Upsaliensia,
         Nova Ser. 1) Uppsala: Almqvist & Wiksell, 1965.
         86p.
              598 items listed in this comprehensive history
         of music printing. Music periodicals indexed:
         AM, AMS Papers, DM, Jahrbuch für Liturgik und
         Hymnologie (#197), MfMG, M&L, MR, SIM, etc.

158(R)   Deutsch, Otto Erich. "Erstdrucke der Musik in
         periodischer Literatur. " MF, 16/1, (1963), 51-2.
              Indexes music, composer and title, in certain
         periodicals of the 17th, 18th and 19th centuries.
         Composers: Gluck, Handel (in London Magazine,
         November 1745); Haydn, Mendelssohn, Mozart,

Purcell (in Gentleman's Journal, between January
1692 and November 1694); Schubert, Schumann,
Wagner, Brahms (in AMZ, July 1864).

159(R) Edmunds, John and Boelzner, Gordon. Some Twentieth Century American Composers: A Selective
Bibliography. New York: New York Public Library, 1959-1960. 2 vols.
Originally appeared in the Bulletin of the
N. Y. P. L., July, August 1959. This has additions. Purpose to bring together published writings by and about representative 20th-century
American composers (conservative, moderate, do-
decaphonic, and experimental). Vol. 1 lists bibliographies for fifteen composers; vol. 2, seventeen
more, with divisions as: Articles by, Articles
about, Articles about works by. Sources: Music
Index (#231), Baker (#123R), Grove (180R), ACA
Bul., MQ, Score, etc.

160   Electronic Music. Washington, D. C.: Music Educators' National Conference, 1968. 97p. and Phono-
disc.
Originally published as the November 1968 issue of the MusEdJ. Includes many periodical
articles.

161   "Electronic Music." Die Reihe, 1, (1958), 1-61.
Articles by Eimert, Stuckenschmidt, Krenek,
Klebe, Boulez, Pousseur, Goeyvaerts, Gredinger,
Stockhausen, Koenig, Meyer-Eppler.

162(R) Endo, Jirosi, comp. Bibliography of Oriental and
Primitive Music. Tokyo: Nanki Music Library,
1929. 62p.
645 items of books and articles. Music periodicals indexed: AfMW, DM, JoMT, MA, MQ,
NZfM, PMA, RM, RMI, SIM, VfMW, ZfMW,
ZIM.

163   Ethnomusicology. Index, vols. 1-10, 1953-1966. Published for the Society for Ethnomusicology by the
Wesleyan University Press, Middletown, Conn.,
1967.
1) Authors, titles, subjects of articles and miscellaneous contributors; 2) Authors, titles and reviews of books; 3) Editors or collectors, titles and

reviews of phonograph records; 4) Editors or collectors, titles and reviewers of films.

164(R)   Ferguson, Donald N.   History of Musical Thought.
         3d ed.   New York: Appleton-Century, 1959.
         675p.
             Bibliography, pp. 639-657, list of books followed
         by a collection of articles in periodical literature.
         Arranged by broad subject headings which include:
         General histories of music, Greek music, Christian
         monody and polyphony, Opera, Biography.   Music
         periodicals indexed: M&L, MQ, MT, PMA.

165   Fink, Michael, comp.   Ed. by Tamara L. Dworsky.
         "Pierre Boulez: A Selective Bibliography. "   CM,
         no. 13 (1972),   135-50.
             Divisions: Writings by Boulez; by Boulez and
         others; Books discussing Boulez among others;
         Articles on Boulez found in periodicals; References
         to specific works by Boulez.

166   _____, comp.   "Anton Webern: Supplement
         to a Basic Bibliography. "   CM, no. 16 (1973),
         103-10.
             Part V, pp. 107-10, articles on Webern in peri-
         odicals.   Music periodicals indexed: American
         Society of University Composers, Proceedings,
         CM, JoMT, MF, MR, Musica, PMA, PNA, Score,
         SMZ, etc.

167(R)   Folstein, Robert L. , comp.   Ed. by Stephen Willis.
         "A Bibliography on Jacques Offenbach: Articles
         on Offenbach Found in Periodicals. "   CM, No. 12
         (1971),   116-28.
             Music periodicals indexed: MO, MQ, MusAmer,
         MusCour, NZfM, OpN, ZfMW.

168(R)   Ford, Wyn K.   Music in England Before 1800:   A
         Select Bibliography.   (Library Association Biblio-
         graphies, 7)   London: The Library Association,
         1967.   128p.
             Literature listed found in the British Museum,
         the Westminster Reference Library of the Central
         Music Library.   Divisions: Music and its environ-
         ment: 1) General, 2) Instruments and instrumental
         music, 3) Folk music, 4) Church music, 5) Social
         conditions, 6) Middle ages, 7) Renaissance, 8) 17th

century, 9) 18th century. Part II: Persons,
General, Individual. Music periodicals indexed:
AfMW, AM, GSJ, MQ, MR, MT, PMA, RBM,
MMR, Music Survey, etc.

169(R)   Foreman, R. L. E. "A Bibliography of the Writings
on Arnold Bax. " CM, no. 10, (1970), 124-40.
Music periodicals indexed: Chesterian (to Fall
1961), M&L, MO, MM, MMR, MT, Music Teacher, Listener, etc.

170(R)   Forrester, F. S. Ballet in England: A Bibliography
and Survey, ca. 1700-June 1966. (Library Association Bibliographies, 9) Foreword by Ivor Guest.
London: Library Association, 1968. 224p.
650 items of books and articles; all articles included are 500 words or over; no claim to complete coverage. Chapter thirteen deals with periodical and newspaper articles concerned chiefly
with ballet (items 647-659). These have descriptive annotations. Music periodicals indexed: The
Listener, MMR, MQ, MR, MT, Musical Standard,
PMA, Sackbut.

171(R)   Galpin Society Journal. Index, vols. 1-5, 1948-1952,
in vol. 5, comp. by Dale Higbee. Vols. 6-10,
1953-1957, comp. by Christopher and Claire
Baines. London, Galpin Society, 1948- . Reprint of vols. 1-19, 1948-1965. Amsterdam:
Swets & Zeitlinger, 1967.

172(R)   Gaskin, L. J. P. , comp. A Select Bibliography of
Music in Africa. Under the direction of Prof. K.
P. Wachsmann, Institute of Ethnomusicology, African Centre Studies, University of California,
Los Angeles. London: International African Institute, 1965. 83p.
Selection made from "all known works containing relevant and significant information on music
in Africa. " Geographically subdivided. Section
on dance; special section on musical instruments.
List of periodicals consulted, pp. 66-70, of which
about seventy are specifically music periodicals
and journals.

173(R)   Gellis, Ronnie. Index of Periodical Literature in
Music. In Progress.

48 Music Periodical Literature

Announced as a continuation of the Bibliography of Periodical Literature in Musicology and Allied Fields (#134R) "to include all periodical literature from October 1, 1940 to September 30, 1941." Approximately 750 entries, on index cards, available on loan. To be published? Source: Checklist of Music Bibliographies and Indexes in Progress and Unpublished. 3d ed. Music Library Association, 1974. (MLA Index Series, 3)

174(R) Gerboth, Walter. An Index to Musical Festschriften and Similar Publications. New York: W. W. Norton, 1969. 188p.
Rev. and enl. version of the index originally printed in Jan LaRue: Aspects of Medieval and Renaissance Music; a Birthday Offering to Gustave Reese, 1966. Organized in three sections: A. List of the Festschriften (under honored individual's name); B. Classified list of the musical articles in the list "A": essays in books or in periodicals; C. Index by author and subject to the articles in "B". Music periodicals indexed include: Canon (Schoenberg), JMP (Friedländer), MM (Schoenberg), MQ (Einstein, Beethoven, Sachs, Stravinsky), RBM (Debussy), RM (Faure, Dukas, Ravel), JAMS & NOTES (Kinkeldey), Score (Stravinsky), Tempo (Bartók).

175(R) Gerlach, John C. and Gerlach, Lana. The Critical Index: A Bibliography on Film in English, 1946-1973, Arranged by Names and Topics. (New Humanistic Research, 1) New York: Teachers' College, Columbia University, Teachers' College Press, 1974.
Guide to articles about directors, producers, actors, critics, screen-writers, cinematographers, specific films and 175 topics dealing with the history, aesthetics and economics of film, etc. Consists of 5,000 items from twenty-two film periodicals (British, Canadian, American), and from over sixty general periodicals. Section on music, pp. 517-520, has four citations on "Music for silents." Periodicals indexed: Films and Filming, Cinema, Hollywood Quarterly, Film Culture, Film Library Quarterly, MQ (one article).

176(R) Godman, Stanley. "A Classified Index of Bach Articles (Including Bach Literature) from 1935-1951."

Hinrichsen's Musical Yearbook, 7, (1952), 392-403.
Music periodicals indexed: Consort, JAMS, Listener, M&L, MQ, MR, MO, MMR, MT, Music Survey, NOTES, PMA, Strad, etc.

177(R) Griffel, Michael. "A Bibliography of the Writings on Ernest Bloch." CM, no. 6 (June 1968), 142-146.
Music periodicals indexed: Etude (to 1957), HF, M&L, MM, MQ, MR, MT, MusAmer, Mus-Cour, RM, SMZ.

178(R) Groeneveld, Dagmar, comp. Ed. by Anne Bagnall. "A Bibliography of the European Harp to 1600." CM, no. 16 (1973), 92-102.
Music periodicals indexed: AfMW, AM, MF, MA, GSJ, NMZ, SIM, etc.

179(R) Grout, Donald Jay. A Short History of Opera. 2d ed. New York: Columbia University, 1965. 852p.
One of the most comprehensive bibliographies of literature on the opera, pp. 586-768, includes both books and articles in the leading European and American periodicals. Music periodicals indexed: AfMW, AMF, AMZ, JAMS, JMP, MA, MD, MQ, MfMG, Musica, NOTES, RM, RMI, RdM, RMB, SMZ, VfMW, ZfMW, SIM, ZIM.

180(R) Grove, Sir George, ed. Grove's Dictionary of Music and Musicians. 5th ed., ed. by Eric Blom. London: Macmillan; New York: St. Martin's Press, 1954. 9 vols. Suppl., v. 10, 1961.
Lists of abbreviations include twenty-one leading European and American (only MQ) periodicals in music. Cited in the bibliographies following subjects or biographies. Only the most worthwhile articles cited.

181(R) Hagopian, Viola L. Italian Ars Nova Music: A Bibliographic Guide to Modern Editions and Related Literature. 2d ed., rev. & enl. (University of California Publications in Music, 7) Berkeley: University of California Press, 1973. 175p.
14th-century Italian music, period from 1325-1425 represented by Magister Piero, Giovanni da

Cascia (or Johannes de Florentia), Jacopo da Bologna, Francesco Landini. Appendix I: Bibliography of works used in this study. Most of the entries have descriptive annotations. Music periodicals indexed: AfMW, AMF, JAMS, JMP, M&L, MD, MF, PMA, RMI, RBM, SIM, Spec, ZfMW, etc.

182(R) Haydon, Glen. Introduction to Musicology: A Survey of the Fields, Systematic and Historical, of Musical Knowledge and Research. New York: Prentice-Hall, 1941. 329p.
Bibliographies at the end of each chapter include articles covering the subject of the chapter. Systematic musicology: acoustics, physiology and psychology in relation to music, musical aesthetics, music theory, pedagogy, comparative musicology. Historical musicology: philosophy of music history, sources, problems and methods of historical research in music. Music periodicals indexed include: AfMW, AM, Journal of the Acoustical Society of America, JMP, MENC, MQ, MTNA Proc, SFQ, SIM, VfMW, ZfMW, ZIM.

183(R) Haywood, Charles. A Bibliography of North American Folklore and Folksong. 2d rev. ed. New York: Dover Publications, 1961. 2 vols.
Vol. 1: The American people north of Mexico: General, Regional, Ethnic, Occupational bibliography, Miscellaneous. Vol. 2: The American Indians north of Mexico, including the Eskimos. Music periodicals indexed: M&L, MM, Music, MusEdJ, MTNA Proc, and various folklore publications.

184   Heaton, Wallace and Hargens, C. W. An Interdisciplinary Index of Studies in Physics, Medicine and Music Related to the Human Voice. Bryn Mawr, Pennsylvania: Theodore Presser, 1968. 61p.
Divided into twelve sections from "anatomical literature related to the vocal cords and singing" to "X-ray studies of the larynx," based upon the needs of research workers, programs and fields such as communication: voice therapy, voice study, laryngeal pathology. Descriptive annotations throughout. Music periodicals indexed include: AMT, MusEdJ, MusJ, NATS Bul, NZfM, etc.

185(R) Henry, Mellinger Edward. A Bibliography for the
        Study of American Folk-Songs with Many Titles
        of Folk-Songs (and Titles That Have to Do with
        Folk-Songs) from Other Lands. London: Mitre
        Press, 1937? 142p.
            Professes to be "not a scientific bibliography. "
        Music and related periodicals indexed include:
        JAF (reference is made to the JAF Index (#90R),
        MusCour, Saturday Review, etc.

186(R) Herzog, George. Research in Primitive and Folk
        Music in the United States; A Survey. (A. C. L. S.
        Bul. , 24) Washington, D. C. : American Council
        of Learned Societies, 1936. 97p.
            Two sections: Primitive music, bibliography,
        pp. 32-41, 592-601, (thirteen periodicals checked);
        Folk music, bibliography, pp. 77-93, 637-53 (four-
        teen periodicals checked).

187   Higbee, Dale. "The Galpin Society, Its Journal and the
        Recorder. " The American Recorder, 6/4, (Fall
        1965), 9-10.
            All articles on the recorder which have appeared
        in the GSJ from vol. 1, March 1948 to vol. 16, May
        1963, with descriptive annotations.

188   _____. "The Recorder and the Galpin Society
        Journal. " The American Recorder, 14/2, (May
        1973), 50-51.
            Continues the bibliography as above. Annotated
        list of articles on the recorder from vol. 17, Feb-
        ruary 1964 to vol. 25, July 1972.

189   High Fidelity Annual Records in Review. Comp. &
        ed. by Peter G. Davis. New York: Charles
        Scribner's Sons; Great Barrington, Mass. : Wyeth
        Press, 1955- .
            Title varies: 1955/1956, Record Annual.
        Recordings listed by composer under categories,
        Vocal, Piano, Organ, Harpsichord, String, etc.
        Reviewer's initials at the end of each review with
        numbering system to indicate issue of High Fideli-
        ty in which review appears.

190(R) Hill, George R. A Preliminary Checklist of Research
        on the Classic Symphony and Concerto to the Time
        of Beethoven (Excluding Mozart and Haydn.) (Music

Indexes and Bibliographies, 2) Hackensack, New
Jersey: Joseph Boonin, 1970. 58p.
Music periodicals indexed include: AfMW,
AMS Bul, FAM, JAMS, M&L, MF, MMR, MQ,
PMA, RdM, RM, RMI, SIM, ZIM, ZfMW.

191(R)   Hinrichsen's Musical Year Book. London: Hinrichsen Edition Ltd., vols. 1-11, 1944-1961.
Ed. by Max Hinrichsen. Volumes published at
irregular intervals under various titles. 1944:
Musical Surveys; vols. for 1945/1946 and 1947/
1948 are combined issues. Other titles: Hinrichsen's Music Yearbook: Music of Our Time; in
1952: Music Book. For various indexes containing periodical articles see: Loewenberg (#211R),
Werner (#288R), Godman (#176R), Mitchell
(#223R).

192(R)   Hinson, Maurice. Guide to the Pianist's Repertoire.
Ed. by Irwin Freundlich. Bloomington: Indiana
University Press, 1973. 831p.
Solo piano literature only. Part I: arranged
by composer, with short biography, lists of works,
etc., and a bibliography which includes periodical
articles. Part II: Bibliography, Appendix, Indexes, Extension of bibliographies in Part I. Indexes: Nationality designation, Arrangers, Trans-
cribers. Music periodicals indexed: AM, AMT,
HF, JAMS, MusJ, M&L, MM, MMR, MQ, MR,
MS, MT, PMA, PNA, SIM, etc.

193(R)   Huerta, Jorge A., ed. A Bibliography of Chicano
and Mexican Dance, Drama and Music. Oxnard,
California: Colegio Quetzalzoatl, 1972. 59p.
Dance, drama, music, with subdivisions: Pre-
Columbian, Mexican, Aztian--books, journals,
plays, newspapers. Music periodicals indexed:
Etude (to 1957), HF, MQ, MusAmer, Musician,
OpN, ARG, and several non-musical journals.

194   "Index of Selected Articles Published in British Musical Periodicals." Ed. by Christel Wallbaum.
Brio: Journal of the United Kingdom Branch of
the International Association of Music Libraries,
Autumn 1965- .
Twenty-three English-language music periodicals
published in England indexed: Church Music, Com-

poser (London), English Folk Dance and Song,
Folk Music Journal, Guitar News, M&L, MO,
MT, Music and Musicians, Music in Education,
MR, Music Teacher, Opera, Organ, Record Col-
lector, Recorded Sound, Recorder and Music Maga-
zine, Royal College of Music Magazine, Sounding,
Strad, Tempo, Trinity College of Music Bul, Welsh
Music.

195(R) "Index to Record Reviews, with Symbols Indicating
Opinions of Reviewers. " Ed. by Kurtz Myers.
NOTES, ser. 2, 5/2, March 1948- . Cumulation
of Index of Record Reviews: Record Ratings; The
Music Library Association's Index of Record Re-
views. New York: Crown, 1956. (Record Re-
views in NOTES, 1948-1956.)
Two indexes: Composer and Subject; Composite
releases arranged by Manufacturer and Number.
Periodicals indexed: American Recorder, Audio,
Consumer Research Bul. , Gramophone, HF, MQ,
Monthly Letter (E. M. G.), New Records, New York
Times (newspaper), Opera, OpN, Pan Pipes (Jour-
nal of Sigma Alpha Iota), Saturday Review, Stereo
Review. This is a major reference work in the
field of discography.

International Folk Music Council, Journal   see
Journal of the International Folk Music Council.

International Inventory of Music Literature   see
RILM Abstracts.

196(R) Jahrbuch der Musikbibliothek Peters. Leipzig: C.
F. Peters, vols. 1-47, 1895-1941.
Each issue gives a list of current new periodicals. Section "Verzeichnis ... Bücher und
Schriften über Musik" did not include periodical
literature; this was taken over by the Bibliographie
des Musikschrifttums (#132R). Obituaries of musicians, date of death and name of periodical where
announcement was made appear in "Totenschau für
das Jahr...." Ed. by Kurt Taut, Rudolf Schwartz,
et al.

197   Jahrbuch für Liturgik und Hymnologie. Vol. 1- .
Kassel: J. Stauda, 1955- .
Each vol. contains two bibliographies: "Litera-

turbericht zur Liturgik," and "Literaturbericht zur
Hymnologie," which survey books and articles,
recently published in Europe and North America,
concerning the origins and development of Chris-
tian liturgy and hymnology. Symbols used are indicated in the first pages of the issue: "Verzeichnis der Abkürzungen." There are frequent critical
annotations. Music periodicals indexed include:
AfMW, AMF, MD, MF, Musica, Musik und Kirche,
ZfMW.

198   Jones, Robert M., ed. "Popular Music: A Survey
        of Books, Folios and Periodicals, with an Index
        to Recently Reviewed Recordings." NOTES, 30/2,
        December 1973- .
            Comp. by the Music Library Association Com-
        mittee on Popular Music. Title varies. Music
        and related periodicals indexed include: Billboard,
        Crawdaddy, Creem, Downbeat, Gramophone, HF,
        HSR, Jazz and Pop, MusJ, and many more.
        Coverage: Country and Western music, Soul, MOR
        ("Middle of the Road"), Musical Comedy, various
        forms of Rock Music. No evaluations noted.

199(R) Journal of the American Musicological Society. Cu-
        mulative Subject and Author Indexes to Articles in
        JAMS, ser. 2, vols. 1-19, 1948-1966. Comp. by
        Carole Franklin. Research Report for Require-
        ments of Master of Library Science, Kent State
        University Graduate School, August 1969. 70p.
        (Unpublished. Available.)
            The first cumulative index to JAMS. Author,
        subject indexes. Source: Checklist of Music Bib-
        liographies and Indexes in Progress and Unpub-
        lished. 3d ed. (Music Library Association Index
        Series, 3) 1974.

200   Journal of the International Folk Music Council.
        Cambridge, England: W. Heffer, vol. 1- .
        1949- . Superseded by Yearbook, Urbana: Uni-
        versity of Illinois Press, 1969- .
            Each issue has a section of publications received
        which includes periodical articles of that or previ-
        ous year. Listed under country: Africa, North
        America, South America, Asia, Europe, etc.,
        describing the periodical and discussing articles on
        folk music appearing therein. Music periodicals

indexed: AM, British Institute of Recorded Sound
Bul., Mens en Melodie, MF, RM, Revista Pro-
Arte Musical, PMA, etc.

201   Journal of the International Folk Music Council. In-
       dex, vols. 1-20, 1949-1968. Comp. by Barbara
       Krader. In progress.
       Source: Checklist of Music Bibliographies and
       Indexes in Progress and Unpublished. 3d ed.
       (Music Library Association Index Series, 3) 1974.
       Publication planned.

202(R) Keats, Sheila. "Reference Articles on American
       Composers: An Index." Juilliard Review, 1,
       (Fall 1954), 21-34.
       Articles on fifty-six American composers. Mu-
       sic periodicals indexed: ACA Bul, M&L, MM,
       MQ, etc.

203(R) Kennedy, Raymond. "A Bibliography of the Writings
       of Mieczyslaw Kolinski." CM, (Spring 1966),
       100-03.
       Music periodicals indexed: DM, ETHNO,
       JIFMC, MQ, JAMS.

204(R) Kinscella, Hazel G., comp. "Americana Index to the
       Musical Quarterly, 1915-1957." JRME, 6/2,
       (Fall 1958), 5-144.
       Index includes information about music which
       has appeared in the MQ since its beginnings to
       1957. Arranged by names, titles, musical com-
       positions, articles, books and a few by topics.
       Author entries list articles by, books by, reviews
       by. Term "Americana" is taken rather broadly.
       Authors and composers included if foreign-born
       and residing in America.

205   Kostka, Stefan M. A Bibliography of Computer Appli-
       cations in Music. (Music Indexes and Bibliogra-
       phies, 7) Hackensack, New Jersey: J. Boonin,
       1974. 61p.
       Music and related periodicals indexed: African
       Music, American Society of University Composers
       Proc., Computers and Automation, Council for
       Research in Music Education Bul, CM, Electronic
       Music, FAM, HSR, HF/MusAmer, JAAC, JoMT,
       Melos, MF, MusEdJ, MusJ, NOTES, RM, Source,
       etc.

206(R) Krohn, Ernst C. The History of Music: An Index
        to the Literature Available in a Selected Group of
        Musicological Publications. (Washington Universi-
        ty Library Studies, 3) St. Louis: Washington Uni-
        versity, 1952. 463p.
            In the field of music history about forty periodi-
        cals are indexed which were published during the
        last eighty-eight years, that is, between 1863 and
        1951. Chiefly German and English. General ar-
        rangement is chronological with sub-divisions by
        subject, from prehistoric times to the present.

207(R) Kunst, Jaap. Ethnomusicology, a Study of Its Nature,
        Its Problems, Methods and Representative Perso-
        nalities, to Which Is Added a Bibliography.   3d
        ed., enl. The Hague: Nijhoff, 1959.   303p.
        Suppl., 1969.
            4,552 items; suppl. added about 500 more.
        Subjects, authors, periodical articles include
        oriental and primitive music, and important ref-
        erences on European folk music. The bibliography
        gives locations to libraries in Western Europe:
        eight Dutch, one British, one Danish, one German,
        one Belgian. Music periodicals indexed: DM,
        MA, MD, MMR, MO, M&L, MM, MF, RM, Mu-
        sic Therapy Journal, etc.

208(R) Lang, Paul Henry. Music in Western Civilization.
        New York: W. W. Norton, 1941. 1,107p.
            Bibliography of literature in all languages in
        one alphabet, pp. 1045-65. Book written along the
        line of the social, political and cultural history of
        Western civilization. Music periodicals indexed
        include: AfMW, AM, MfMG, M&L, MQ, MT,
        JMP, RM, RMI, SIM, VfMW, ZfMW.

209(R) Lehman, Paul R. "A Selected Bibliography of Works
        on Music Testing." JRME, 17/4, (1969), 427-42.
            Periodical articles on "Experimental texts and
        studies," pp. 431-34; "Studies concerning published
        tests," pp. 434-39.

210(R) Lieberman, Frederic. Chinese Music: An Annotated
        Bibliography. (Bibliographies and Research Aids,
        Series A, No. 1) New York: Society for Asian
        Music, 1970. 157p. Suppl. no. 1, 1973.
            Chinese music, dance, drama. Excluded: de-

tails of acting technique, literary aspects of opera
texts, publications in Oriental languages. Some
emphasis on theory. 1,483 items, books and articles, listed. Index to journals, pp. 125-48, include 387 magazines, of which 106 are music.
Most of the titles are annotated.

211(R) Loewenberg, Alfred, comp. "Bibliography of Books
and Articles on Music. " Hinrichsen's Musical
Year Book, 1/(1944), 247; 2/3 (1945-1946), 356-
95; 4/5 (1947-1948), 495-533.
Subject List; Personal List. Covers periodical
articles from January 1942 to the end of 1946.
Music periodicals indexed: Gramophone, Keynote,
Listener, MD, MM, MMR, M&L, MQ, MR, MO,
MT, NOTES, Organ, Music Teacher, Radio Times,
Strad, Tempo, and some non-musical periodicals.

212   Logan, Kathryn and Walker, Richard L. Checklist
of Music Related Articles Appearing in Scholarly,
Non-Music Journals. In progress.
"Selected list of articles from those periodical
indexes concerned primarily with scholarly jour-
nals, that is, British Humanities Index (#54R),
Social Sciences and Humanities Index (#104R),
Sociological Index, etc. Indexed from 1970.
Author/title arrangement. 150 entries. Source:
Checklist of Music Bibliographies and Indexes in
Progress and Unpublished. 3d ed. (Music Li-
brary Association Index Series, 3) 1974.

213(R) Lowens, Irving. "Writings about Music in the Periodicals of American Transcendentalism (1835-1850). "
JAMS, 10/2, (Summer 1957), 71-85.
Music articles appearing in seven Transcendental periodicals between 1835 and 1850. Appendix
is a check-list of the articles in these periodicals
(see #21R for list). Items 1-23 have many translations by John Sullivan Dwight of articles from
the Deutsche Schnellpost; total of 183 items include
110 articles by Dwight in The Harbinger; other
writers of the period were Charles A. Dana,
George W. Curtis.

214(R) MacArdle, Donald W. Beethoven Abstracts. Detroit:
Information Coordinators, Inc. , 1973. 448p.
Abstracts or summaries of periodical articles

on Beethoven, from the 18th century to the present. Divisions: 1) Primary music periodicals indexed: thirty-eight titles, majority German, a
few French, three from the United States (JAMS,
MQ, NOTES); 2) Secondary periodicals indexed:
eleven titles, majority nonmusical (with two exceptions): MusAmer, MusCour. Indexes: General, Author, to Compositions, of Correspondents.

215   McAllester, David Park, comp. Readings in Ethno-
        musicology. New York: Johnson Reprint Corp.,
        1971. 370p.
            Reprint of articles appearing in: American
        Anthropologist, ETHNO, African Music, Folklore
        and Folk Music Archivist, JAF, Journal of Music
        Therapy, etc.

216   Maleady, Antoinette O., comp. Record and Tape Re-
        views Index, 1971- . Metuchen, New Jersey:
        Scarecrow Press, 1972- .
            Replacement for discontinued Polart Index
        (#251); companion to High Fidelity Records in Re-
        view (#189). Reviews of classical music on discs,
        tapes and cassettes, including reviews of spoken
        recordings. Arranged by composers, music in
        collections (anonymous works included) spoken
        recordings. Performer index. Qualitative evalua-
        tion from ++ (excellent) to - (poor) and * (no eva-
        luation. About twenty periodicals indexed. Music
        periodicals indexed: American Recorder, ARG,
        Gramophone, HF, HiFi News (London), MusJ,
        New Records, OpN, Opera, Stereo Review, and
        several non-musical periodicals.

217(R) Marks, Paul F. Bibliography of Literature Concern-
        ing Yemenite-Jewish Music. (Detroit Studies in
        Music Bibliography, 27) Detroit: Information Co-
        ordinators, 1973. 50p.
            Section, pp.11-29, deals with music, anthro-
        pology, sociology, and history concerned with the
        Jewish tradition within the Islamic culture of the
        Yemen. Music periodicals indexed include: AM,
        Allgemeine Literatur der Musik, ETHNO, Jewish
        Music Forum Bul., Journal of the Folk Song So-
        ciety (London), JIFMC, MTNA Proc., Musica He-
        braica, SIM, ZfMW.

218(R) Mathiesen, Thomas J. Bibliography of Sources for
        the Study of Ancient Greek Music. (Music Biblio-
        graphies and Indexes, 10) Hackensack, New Jer-
        sey: J. Boonin, 1974. 59p.
            Alphabetically arranged by author and theorist.
        Includes listings of books, articles, theses, dis-
        sertations and other sources: 949 items. Music
        periodicals indexed: AM, AMF, DM, ETHNO,
        JAMS, JMP, MF, MfMG, MQ, MR, Music
        (1892-), Musica, NMZ, RBM, RM, RMI, SIM,
        ZfMW, etc.

219(R) Merriam, Alan P. "An Annotated Bibliography of
        African and African-Derived Music Since 1936."
        Africa, 21/4, (October 1951), 319-29.
            An extension of Varley's African Native Music
        (#280R). Lists books and articles published
        since 1936 on African music, with some earlier
        references not in Varley. Bibliography in two
        parts: Works checked personally in libraries in
        the Chicago area; Works unavailable in this area.
        Music periodicals indexed: AMF, Boletín Latino-
        Americano de Musica, Etude, JAMS, Music Sur-
        vey, MM, MusJ, MusAmer, JIFMC, DM, Revista
        de Estudios Musicale, Revue Grégorienne, Zeit-
        schrift für Instrumentanbau.

220(R) _____ . The Anthropology of Music. Evanston,
        Illinois: Northwestern University Press, 1964.
        358p.
            Essays on various aspects of ethnomusicology.
        References cited, pp. 321-43. Many non-musical
        periodicals of ethnic, anthropological, psychologi-
        cal basis indexed. Music and related periodicals
        indexed: African Music, JAF, JAAC, Journal of
        Music Therapy, JAMS, MQ, MusJ, MusEdJ, MM,
        MTNA Proc., SFQ.

221(R) _____ . Bibliography of Jazz. (Publications of the
        American Folklore Society Series, vol. 4) Phila-
        delphia: American Folklore Society, 1954. 145p.
            Extension of two articles by Merriam, "A Short
        Bibliography of Jazz," Record Changer, 9, (July/
        August 1950), 33-5; and NOTES 10/2, (March
        1953), 202-10. Not intended to be "selective,"
        but makes no claim to completeness. Divisions:
        1) 3,324 individual entries arranged by author, in-

cluding periodical and newspaper articles; 2) list
of magazines which have been devoted wholly or
in considerable part to jazz music (many are now
defunct, some were published for only a very short
period of time). Indexes: Subject; various periodicals cited (113 jazz periodicals). Music periodicals indexed: 122; Non-musical: 165.

222   Messenger, Ruth Ellis, comp. "Hymns in Periodical
         Literature." The Hymn, 1/4-14/3, (October
         1950-July 1963).
              Listed in issues irregularly. Music periodicals
         indexed include: Catholic Choirmaster, Journal of
         Church Music, Music Ministry, Response.

223(R)   Mitchell, Donald. "The Emancipation of the Dis-
         sonance: A Selected Bibliography of the Writings
         of Composers, Theorists, and Critics of the So-
         Called 'Contemporary Music,' Preceded by Short
         Biographies of Twelve-Tone Composers." Hin-
         richsen's Musical Year Book, 7, (1952), 141-152.
              Thirty-nine music periodicals indexed including:
         AM, Chesterian, DM, The Listener (London), MO,
         MQ, MR, MT, Canon (Australia), M&L, MM,
         MMR, Melos, RM, NMZ, SMZ, Sackbut, Tempo.

224(R)   Modern Music. Index, vols. 1-12, November 1924-
         June 1935. Comp. by Joel Lifflander. New York:
         League of Composers, 1924-1946.
              Indexes: Subjects, Authors and Articles, Illus-
         trations, Table of Concerts (by issues).

225(R)   _____. Index, vols. 1-23, 1924-1946. New York:
         AMS Press, 1973.
              Arranged by author, title, major topics.

226(R)   _____. Index: Published by the League of Com-
         posers, 1924-1946: an Analytic Index. Ed. by
         William Lichtenwanger and C. Lichtenwanger.
         New York: AMS Press, 1975.
              Probably the same as above (#225R).

227(R)   Modisett, Katherine C. "Bibliography of Sources,
         1930-1952, Relating to the Teaching of Choral
         Music in Secondary Schools." JRME, 3, (Spring
         1955), 52-60.
              Classified bibliography. Non-musical periodi-

cals indexed: <u>Education, College Teachers'
Record, Review of Education Research, Journal
of Applied Psychology.</u> Music periodicals indexed:
<u>M&L, MENC Yearbook, MusEdJ, MusJ, Musicolo-
gy, MTNA Proc.</u>

228(R) <u>Music and Letters. Index, vols. 1-40, 1920-1959.</u>
Comp. by Eric Blom and Jack Westrup. London:
Oxford University Press, 1962. 140p.

229 <u>Music Article Guide: An Annotated Comprehensive
Quarterly Reference Guide to Significant Signed
Feature Articles in American Music Periodicals.</u>
Vol. 1- . Philadelphia, Penna. : Music Article
Guide, Winter 1965/1966- .
Indexes approximately 170 American periodicals,
all in English, from scholarly and semi-scholarly
music journals as JAMS, MD, MQ, to house or-
gans of local and/or ephemeral worth as <u>After
Dark, Bluegrass Music News, Joy Magazine.</u> Majority of the articles concerned primarily with music education and with the music industry. Subject, author, title listings. Author entry refers to
the title, under topical subject, which gives a short
summary of the article.

<u>Music Book</u> see <u>Hinrichsen's Musical Year Book.</u>

230(R) <u>Music Educators' Journal: A Subject Index to the Music Educators' Journal, 1934-1949.</u> Comp. by
Russell C. Cummings. Unpublished Masters' Thesis, School of Education, University of Southern
California, 1949. 129ℓ.
Coverage: vols. 21-35, September 1934-July
1949. Subject headings are broad as, "Music History, " "America, Music in, " "Musicology, " but
there are many cross-references to make the index
more useful. No author or title index. General
outline and index is an alphabetical list of subject
headings.

231 <u>The Music Index; The Key to Current Music Periodical Literature.</u> Vol. 1/1- . Detroit: Information Service, 1949- .
Subject-author guide to about 350 (in 1976) current periodicals from the United States, England,
Canada, Australia and nineteen non-English lan-

guage countries. Entries are in the language of
the country of origin. Published in twelve monthly numbers, with an annual cumulation. Reviews
are listed under "Book Reviews." Ranges in aspects of the music field from musicology to the
retailing of music. Indexes music periodicals
completely and several related periodicals selectively, as JAAC, JAF.

232(R)   Music Library Association, Notes.   Index, first
         series, no. 1-15, July 1934-December 1942, comp.
         by Frank C. Campbell.   Unpublished.
              Index, second series, vol. 1- .   December
         1943- .   Comp. by Frank C. Campbell, Ralph
         Moritz in separate indexes issued biennially,
         through vol. 20, 1963.   Now indexed at end of
         each volume, by Ruth A. Solie, June 1974- .

233(R)   Music Teachers' National Association, Proceedings.
         Indexes, vols. 1-40, 1906-1946.
              Vols. 1-10, 1906-1915, in Vol. 10; Vols-10-23,
         1916-1929, in Vol. 24; Vols. 24-31, 1930-1936, in
         Vol. 32; Vols. 32-40, 1937-1946, in Vol. 41.

234(R)   Musica Disciplina; A Journal of the History of Music.
         Rome: American Institute of Musicology, March
         1946- .
              Published March 1946-June 1947 under title:
         Journal of Renaissance and Baroque Music.   With
         vol. 10, 1956, became a Year-book.   Indexes,
         each issue, music periodical articles relating to
         the Renaissance and Baroque periods of music:
         AfMW, AM, FAM, GSJ, JAMS, M&L, MF, MMR
         (to December 1960), MQ, NOTES, Score (to June
         1962), SMZ, Strad, etc.

235(R)   _____ .   Index, vols. 1-20, 1946-1966.   Ed. by
         Thomas L. Noblitt.   Rome: American Institute
         of Musicology, 1969?
              Indexes: Authors, Subjects.

236(R)   Musical Quarterly.   Cumulative Index, vols. 1-45,
         1915-1959.   Comp. by Herbert K. Goodkind.   New
         York: Goodkind Indexes, 1960.   Suppl. , vol. 46-
         58, 1960-1962.

237(R)   _____ .   Subject Index of Articles Published in the
         Musical Quarterly, vols. 11-34, 1925-1948, Includ-

ing Annotations of Articles Published 1940-1948.
Comp. by Worth A. Blair.   Unpublished Master's
Thesis, School of Music, University of Southern
California, 1949. 116ℓ.
Indexed under author, subject, by country, followed by an index of general musical subjects not
associated with a particular country or person.
315 articles from vols.11-26, 1940-1948, are annotated.

238(R) Die Musik in Geschichte und Gegenwart.   Ed. by
Friedrich Blume.   Kassel: Bärenreiter, 1949-
1967. 15 vols. Suppl. in progress.
Detailed bibliographical references include selected articles from a large number of periodicals,
music and non-musical, in many languages. From
the list of abbreviations, music periodicals indexed
include: AfMW, AMZ, DM, JMP, MfMG, M&L,
MQ, Musik und Kirche, RM, RMI, RdM, SIM,
VfMW, ZfMW, ZIM.

239(R) National Association for Music Therapy.   Bibliography
on Music Therapy.   Comp. by Ray Green, et al.
Ed. by Helen Ann Dinklage.   Chicago, National
Association for Music Therapy, 1952. 41p.
Excerpt from the Association's Proceedings.
Contents: Music therapy prior to 1900, Experi-
mental studies, Music in hospitals, Music in in-
dustry, Music for children--education, Music for
exceptional children.   Music periodicals indexed
include: Educational Music Magazine, Etude, MQ,
Overture, MusEdJ, JAAC, Pan Pipes, Hospital
Music Newsletter, MTNA Proc.

240(R) Nelson, Robert U. and Rubsamen, Walter H., comp.
"Literature on Music in Film and Radio."   Hollywood Quarterly: Annual Communication Bibliography, vol.1, Suppl., 1946, 40-45.
Reprinted, with additions, in Hinrichsen's Musical Year Book (#191R) with title "Bibliography of
Books and Articles of Music in Film and Radio."
Material from general bibliographies on film and
radio, standard indexes, periodical literature, references in books and articles.   Selective, covering
literature since 1930.   Music and related periodicals indexed: Arts and Architecture, Cinema
Quarterly, M&L, MQ, MM, MTNA Proc., Theatre
Arts, etc.

241(R)   Nettl, Bruno, comp. "Articles on Folk, Primitive
         and Oriental Music in the Musical Quarterly, vols.
         1-41, 1915-1955. " ETHNO, no. 10, (May 1957),
         15-22.
             Subject headings: General and miscellaneous,
         English and Anglo-American, Western Europe,
         Eastern Europe, African and New World Negro,
         American Indian, Other primitives, Oriental.

242(R)   _____. Music in Primitive Culture. Cambridge:
         Harvard University Press, 1956. 200p.
             Bibliography, pp. 145-166, with short, descript-
         ive annotations. Divisions of works of/on: Gen-
         eral and theoretical interest, American Indian mu-
         sic, African and New World negro music, Asiatic
         and Oceanic music, Musical instruments, Indicat-
         ing relationships between primitive music and other
         areas of study, Bibliographies and works of biblio-
         graphic interest, Periodicals devoted largely to
         primitive music. Music and related periodicals
         indexed: Africa, AM, American Anthropologist,
         JAF, JAMS, JMP, MF, MQ, NOTES, SIM, ZfMW,
         etc.

243(R)   _____. "Musicological Studies in American Ethno-
         logical Journals. " NOTES, 12/2, (March 1955),
         205-9.
             119 entries arranged in seven categories: Gen-
         eral articles, theory of comparative musicology,
         field work, etc. ; American Indian music; Anglo-
         American and American Negro folk music; Other
         primitive music; Other folk music; Language and
         music; Musical instruments. Studies of Anglo-
         American and North American Indian music pre-
         dominate. Most of the articles are from the folk-
         lore journals and the American Anthropologist,
         dealing with some phase of comparative musicology.
         Music and related periodicals indexed: American
         Anthropologist (from 1899 and earlier series,
         1888-1898), Anthropological Quarterly (from 1928),
         JAF (from 1888), Southwestern Journal of Anthro-
         pology (from 1945), Western Folklore (from 1942).

244(R)   _____. Reference Materials in Ethnomusicology:
         A Bibliographic Essay. 2d ed. , rev. (Detroit
         Studies in Music Bibliography, 1) Detroit: Infor-
         mation Coordinators, Inc. , 1967. 40p.

Emphasis is on information regarding the music
of non-literate or primitive cultures and of the
oriental high cultures. Treatment of folk music
is somewhat superficial. Arrangement is classified. List of publications cited, pp. 30-40. Music and related periodicals indexed include:
Amer. Anthropologist, Africa, English Folk Dance
and Song, ETHNO, GSJ, JAF, JIFMC, JAMS,
NOTES, etc.

245(R)   New York Public Library. Reference Dept. Dictionary Catalog of the Music Collection. Vols. 1-
33. Boston: G. K. Hall, 1964-1971. Cumulative supplements (New York Public Library. Research Libraries), vols. 1-10. Boston, G. K.
Hall, 1973.
Holdings of the Music Division of the N. Y. P. L.
of books, pamphlets and musical scores. In one
alphabet with many pertinent cross-references.
Indexes many music periodicals in all languages
under appropriate subject headings.

246(R)   Newman, William S. Sonata in the Baroque Era.
Rev. ed. (Norton Library, N622) Chapel Hill:
University of North Carolina Press, 1966. 463p.
The first vol. of a "History of the Sonata Idea. "
Coverage is "loosely" 1600-1750; geographically:
Italy, Germany, England, France. Part I: Gen-
eral nature of the Baroque sonata explored; Part
II: Specific production of individual composers.
"Addenda 1966" lists by page, additional notes and
references. Bibliography, pp. 407-449, indexes
many periodical articles on music.

247(R)   _____ . Sonata in the Classic Era; The Second
Volume of a History of the Sonata Idea. (Norton
Library, N623) Chapel Hill: University of North
Carolina Press, 1963. 897p.
Coverage shortly before 1740 to the last sonatas
of Beethoven and Clementi, completed after 1820.
Part I: Summary, over all view of the Classic
sonata--its meanings, uses, spread, settings and
forms; Part II: Detailed survey of individual com-
posers and their works. Bibliography, pp. 810-869.
Music periodicals indexed: AfMW, AM, AMZ,
DM, FAM, MF, M&L, MMR, MQ, MR, RaM.

248(R) _____. The Sonata Since Beethoven; The Third
        and Final Volume of a History of the Sonata Idea.
        (Norton Library, N624) 2d ed. New York: W.
        W. Norton, 1972. 858p.
            Coverage, beginning of the Romantic period to
        the late-Romantics (Rachmaninoff, R. Strauss,
        Elgar, Nielsen, d'Indy, etc.). Part I: over-all
        view, surveying the problem, meaning, use,
        spread, scoring and form of the sonata since Beet-
        hoven; Part II: more detailed views, individual
        composers and their sonatas, region by region.
        "Addenda 1972" lists by page in text additional
        notes and references. Bibliography, pp. 780-837.
        Music periodicals indexed: AfMW, AM, AMZ,
        DM, Chesterian, Dwight's Journal of Music, JAAC,
        JMP, MF, NMZ, NOTES, NZfM, PMA, RaM,
        RBM, RdM, SIM, SMZ, Strad, SZMW, Tempo,
        ZfMW, ZIM, etc.

249(R) The Organ. Index to All Articles, 1921-1970. Comp.
        by Betty Matthews. Bournemouth: K. Mummery,
        1970.
            Author, subject and location indexes, cross-ref-
        erenced with the author index to trace issue and
        page number of article.

250   Poladian, Sirvart, comp. "Index to Music Necrology."
        NOTES, 22/4, -June 1966- .
            Further compilers: D. L. Hudson, P. Matusky,
        Janet Pinkowitz (June 1975-). Appears annually
        in the June issues. Obituaries of composers and
        musicians in music periodicals: AM, Boletin In-
        teramericano de Música, Courrier Musical de
        France, JAMS, Musica, MT, Musik und Kirche,
        New York Times (newspaper), NZfM, Opera (Lon-
        don), OpN, Das Orchester, SMZ.

251   Polart Index to Record Reviews, Including Tapes.
        Detroit, Michigan: Polart, 1961-1967? Arranged
        by name of composer, "collections" and "miscel-
        laneous." Section on "Pop and Jazz" and "Tapes."
        Indexes critical reviews of recordings and tapes
        published in eleven English-language periodicals.
        Replaced by Maleady (#216).

        Proceedings of the Royal Musical Association
        (PAM) see Royal Musical Association, Proceed-
        ings.

252(R) La Rassegna Musicale. Indice Generale delle Annate,
        vols. 1-22, 1928-1952. Comp. by Riccardo Allorto.
        Torino, Roggero and Tortia, 1953.

253(R) Reaney, Gilbert. "Bibliography of Music Articles
        Concerning the Middle Ages, Renaissance and
        Baroque." The Listener, vol. 36-54, August
        1946-1955. Reprinted in MD, vol. 10, 1956, 220-4.
        The Listener (English weekly, 1929-) contains
        reprints of talks broadcast by the BBC. At the
        end of each issue are music articles by specialists
        which are to be broadcast during the succeeding
        week. Since August 1946 these articles have be-
        come increasingly important. Well-known English
        authors and their articles are listed in this biblio-
        graphy, such names as: Martin Cooper, Thurston
        Dart, Wilfrid Mellers, Ernst Meyer, Gilbert
        Reaney, Hans Redlich, Alec Robertson, Denis
        Stevens, Egon Wellesz, Jack Westrup, etc.

254(R) Reese, Gustave. Fourscore Classics of Music Liter-
        ature. New York: Liberal Arts Press, 1957.
        91p.
        A guide to selected original sources on theory
        and other writings on music not available in Eng-
        lish, with descriptive sketches and bibliographical
        references. From Ptolemy, second century, to
        Alois Hába (1927), eighty items. Music periodi-
        cals indexed: AfMW, AM, JAMS, Kirchenmusi-
        kalisches Jahrbuch, M&L, MD, MfMG, MQ, SIM,
        VfMW, ZfMW.

255(R) _____. Music in the Middle Ages, With an Intro-
        duction on the Music of Ancient Times. New
        York: W. W. Norton, 1940. 502p.
        Period covered, ancient times to the middle of
        the 15th century. Bibliography, pp. 425-63, divided
        into individual chapters, in two parts: books and
        articles; music collections and facsimiles. Music
        periodicals indexed indicated by symbols, include:
        AfMW, AM, MfMG, MA, MQ, PMA, RdM, RM,
        SIM, ZfMW, ZIM.

256(R) _____. Music in the Renaissance. 2d ed. New
        York, W. W. Norton, 1959. 1,022p.
        Coverage, 15th and 16th centuries. Bibliogra-
        phy, pp. 884-946, lists sources by symbols. In-

cludes many music periodical articles under author
and cites periodicals with date of first issue.

257(R)   Refardt, Edgar.   Verzeichnis der Aufsätze zur Musik
in den nicht-musikalischen Zeitschriften der Uni-
versitäts-Bibliothek Basel, abgeschlossen auf den
1.Januar 1924.   Leipzig: Breitkopf & Härtel,
1925.   105p.
Period covered, about 1700-1925.   Indexes music writings in over 550 non-musical newspapers
and periodicals in the University Library at Basel.
International in scope but predominantly those in
the German language.   Arranged by subject, by
country for historical articles, biographical section by biographee (about thirty pages).   No table
of contents or index of authors or titles.

258   Die Reihe; A Periodical Devoted to Developments in
Contemporary Music.   Bryn Mawr, Theodore
Presser, 1958-1968?
English translation of the German Die Reihe
which began in 1955.   Each vol. contains essays
on a special topic, as vol.1 on electronic music
(#161).

259   Reisner, Robert George, comp.   The Literature of
Jazz; A Selective Bibliography.   2d ed.   New
York: New York Public Library, 1959.   63p.
Preliminary edition in the N. Y. P. L. Bul.,
March-May 1954.   850 periodical articles in a
selective list of magazine references, pp. 31-59,
with full bibliographic information on each.   Mu-
sic periodicals indexed include: Etude, M&L,
RM, MM, Sackbut, Musician, SchMus, etc.

260(R)   Renaissance News: An Index of Articles and Book
Reviews Pertaining to Music, Including a Selection
of Articles on Related Subjects.   Comp. by Bar-
bara R. Greener.   Vol.1- .   Spring 1948- .
In Progress.
Source: Checklist of Music Bibliographies and
Indexes in Progress and Unpublished.   2d ed.
(Music Library Association Index Series, 3) 1969.
To be published in this series.

Répertoire International de Littérature Musicale
see   RILM Abstracts.

261(R) Revue de Musicologie. Paris: Société Française de
        Musicologie, Librairie Fischbacher, t.1- , annee
        1- . 1917- .
        Title varies: Bulletin de la Société de Musicol-
        ogie, vol.1-2, no. 1-10, 1917-1921; Revue de
        Musicologie, 1922 (new series); suspended 1939,
        resumed in 1945, no. 73/74- , vol.27- . "Som-
        maires des périodiques musicaux français et étran-
        gers" appears in second issue of each annual vol.
        It indexes selected journals devoted to musicology,
        published in France, in major non-French journals,
        arranged by country of publication. Later it was
        listed as "Périodiques Congrès et Mélanges" comp.
        by Mme. Elisabeth Lebeau (Bibliothèque Nationale).
        Music periodicals indexed: Le Ménestrel Caecilia,
        Caecilia (Strasbourg), Revue Grégorienne, M&L,
        MQ, RMI, La Tribune de St. Gervais. In 1964
        added: FAM, AM, JIFMC, etc.

262(R) Rhodes, Willard. "North American Music: A Biblio-
        graphical Survey of Anthropological Theory."
        NOTES, 10/1, (December 1952), 33-45.
        Articles on the music and dance by well-known
        authors in the field as: George Herzog, Alice
        Cunningham Fletcher, Frances Densmore, Helen
        H. Roberts, Carl Stumpf in: American Anthro-
        pologist, JAF, MM, MQ, Psychological Reviews.

263   RILM Abstracts of Music Literature (International
        Repertory of Musical Literature). Vol.1- .
        New York: City University of New York, 1967- .
        Répertoire International de Littérature Musi-
        cale: an abstracted, computer-indexed bibliography
        of scholarly current literature on music. All in
        English (foreign titles are translated). Headings:
        Reference and Research Materials, Ethnomusicolo-
        gy, Instruments and Voice, Performance Practice
        and Notation, Theory and Analysis, Pedagogy, Mu-
        sic and other Disciplines, and many sub-headings.
        Each fourth issue cumulates the year's lists.
        Category I: about two dozen music periodicals
        fully abstracted; Category II: partially abstracted
        periodicals; Category III: non-music journals (and
        some music) occasionally abstracted.

264(R) Rivista Musicale Italiana. Indici dei vols.1-20, 1894-
        1913. Comp. by Luigi Parigi. Torino: Fratelli

Bocca, 1917.
Indici dei vols. 21-36, 1913-1928. Comp. by
A. Salvatori and B. Concina. Torino, 1931.
Indici dei vols. 36-57, 1929-1955. Comp. by
Francesco Degrada. Firenzi: Olschki, 1966.
(Quaderna dell Rivista Italiana di Musicologica a
cura della Società Italiana di Musicologie, I)

265(R) Royal Musical Association, Proceedings. Index to
        Papers Read Before the Members, 1874-1944.
        London: Leeds, 1948.
        Subject and author index to the first seventy
        vols. of the PMA. Comp. by Alfred Loewenberg
        and Rupert Erlebach.

266   Sacred Music. Vol. 1- . Latrobe, Penna.: Church
        Music Association of America, 1965- . Continu-
        ation of Caecilia, 1874-1964, and of Catholic
        Choirmaster, vols. 1-50, 1914-1964.
        Reviews of the arts include periodical articles
        section, comp. by various editors, etc. of the
        periodical. Music accompanies some issues.
        Music periodical articles critically annotated
        from: Choral Journal, Journal of Church Music,
        Music Ministry, Music--The AGO-RCCO Magazine,
        Singende Kirche, Musicae Sacrae Ministerium,
        Church Music, Worship and Liturgical Arts.

267(R) Sasse, Konrad, comp. Händel Bibliographie; unter
        Verwendung des im Händel-Jahrbuch 1933 von
        Kurt Taut Veröffentlichten Verzeichnisses des
        Schrifttums über George Friedrich Händel. Abge-
        schlossen im Jahre 1961. Leipzig: VEB Deuts-
        cher Verlag für Musik, 1963. 352p. Supp.,
        1962-1965.
        Basis of the bibliography is the Händel-Jahrbuch
        1933-1961, but beyond the German-speaking world.
        Händel's life and works, pp. 9-322. Author index.
        Many music periodicals checked, including: MO,
        MQ, MT, RaM, RMI, RM, MMR, etc.

268(R) Sendrey, Alfred. Bibliography of Jewish Music.
        New York: Columbia University, 1951. 404p.
        About 10, 000 titles. Part I is concerned with
        writings on Jewish music; Part II is a classified
        list of Jewish music. Author indexes for both
        parts. Music periodicals indexed for Part I:

AfMW, AMZ, Der Anbruch, DM, Jewish Music
Journal, MM, MMR, MQ, MT, MusAmer, Mus-
Cour, NZfM, RaM, RM, SIM, VfMW, ZfMW,
ZIM.

269   Spector, Johanna, comp.   "Articles and Reviews on
       Folk and Art Music of Central Asiatic Peoples
       from Sovetskaya Muszka, 1950-1955. " ETHNO,
       3 (January 1959), 18-22.
       Sovetskaya Muszka is a monthly magazine in
       Russia, issued by composers of the U. S. S. R. and
       the Committee for Art and the Ministry of Arts
       of the U. S. S. R. The 1950-1955 issues are listed
       under: General, Kazakhstan, Kirghizistan, Tad-
       shikistan, Turkmenistan, Uzbekistan, the five
       Soviet republics formerly known under the name
       of Turkestan.

270(R) Speculum: An Index of Musically Related Articles
       and Book Reviews, vols. 1-43, 1926-1968. (Music
       Library Association Index Series, 9) Comp. by
       Arthur S. Wolff. Ann Arbor, Michigan: Music
       Library Association, 1970. 31p.
          Articles listed by author and subject, with sup-
       plementary entries for reviewers and titles (by
       catchword); individual publications in collective re-
       views are given supplementary entries for author
       or editor and title.

271(R) Standifer, James A. , and Reeder, Barbara. Source
       Book of African and Afro-American Materials for
       Music Educators. (Contemporary Music Project,
       7) Chicago, Music Educators National Conference,
       1972. 147p.
          Part I: African music. Articles on music,
       pp. 6-8, indexes: ETHNO, JIFMC, Composer,
       African Music, and several non-music periodicals;
       articles on dance, p. 10, indexes: African Music,
       ETHNO, etc. Periodicals regularly containing ar-
       ticles on African music, p. 13. Part II: Afro-
       American music, pp. 61-7, indexes: Jazz Monthly,
       Record Changer, ETHNO, MusEdJ, JAMS, MQ,
       JRME, etc. All are annotated. Two appendices:
       Classified Name List; General Bibliographic Ref-
       erences.

       Subject Index to Periodicals see British Humani-
       ties Index.

272(R)   Sunderman, Lloyd Frederick. Historical Foundations
         of Music Education in the United States. Metuchen,
         New Jersey: Scarecrow Press, 1971. 453p.
             Section nine, pp. 417-33, articles from American
         periodical history. Music periodicals indexed in-
         clude: Etude (to 1957), MusEdJ, Music Supervi-
         sors' Journal, SchMus.

273   Supicic, Ivo, comp. "Sociology of Music--Selected
         Bibliography, 1950-1970. " International Review
         of the Aesthetics and Sociology of Music, 1/2,
         (December 1970), 229-40.
             Indexes articles on subjects of aesthetics and
         sociology of music which have appeared in this
         periodical and on these subjects from 1950 to
         1970 in over 100 publications. Music periodicals
         indexed: AfMW, AM, JAAC, JAF, JIFMC, JRME,
         Kirchenmusikalisches Jahrbuch, Musica, NZfM,
         MF, MQ, RbM, RM, SMZ.

274(R)   Surian, Elvidio. Checklist of Writings on 18th-Cen-
         tury French and Italian Opera (Excluding Mozart)
         (Music Indexes and Bibliographies, 3) Hackensack,
         New Jersey: Joseph Boonin, 1970. 121p.
             Based on Grout (#179R), adding about 400 more
         entries. Includes articles on librettos, librettists,
         theatrical production; excludes literature, etc. on
         Mozart's operas, Singspiel, ballad operas. Gen-
         eral bibliography includes histories of the drama
         and literature. Music periodicals indexed: thirty-
         six titles of periodicals; one non-musical title:
         Modern Language Association of America, Pro-
         ceedings.

275(R)   Tennessee Folklore Society, Bulletin. Index to the
         First Thirty Volumes. Tennessee Folklore So-
         ciety, 31/3, (1965), 68-97.

276   Thieme, Darius L., comp. African Music: A Brief-
         ly Annotated Bibliography. Washington, D. C. :
         Library of Congress, 1964. 55p.
             Section A incorporates an article by Thieme,
         "Selected Bibliography of Periodical Articles on
         the Music of the Native Peoples of Sub-Saharan
         Africa. " African Music, 3/1, (1962), 103-10,
         which also was published by the Catholic Univer-
         sity of America, Washington, D. C. , 1963. 513

articles in 144 periodicals listed, mainly published
between 1950 and 1963; about thirty-five of these
are music periodicals, annotated.

277(R) Thompson, Annie Figueroa, comp. An Annotated
        Bibliography of Writings about Music in Puerto
        Rico. (Music Library Association Index Series,
        12) Ann Arbor, Michigan: Music Library Asso-
        ciation, 1975. 34p.
        Includes references to books, sections and
        chapters of books, dissertations and journal ar-
        ticles. 304 items date from 1844 to 1972, with
        a few short annotations. Arranged alphabetically
        by author. Subject index. Music and related
        periodicals indexed include (in English): JAF,
        JAMS, International Musician, Music News,
        MusAmer, MusEdJ, and many.more articles in
        Spanish periodicals.

278   Toledo, Ohio. Museum of Art. The Printed Note,
        500 Years of Music Printing and Engraving. Ex-
        hibition, January 14-February 24, 1957. Toledo:
        Museum of Art, 1957. 144p.
        Bibliography of sixty-seven items, includes
        thirty-one periodical articles, of which twenty
        are music from such as: MfMG, JAMS, AfMW,
        AMS Papers, MQ, MT, MR, NOTES, Tijdschrift
        voor Musiekwetenschap.

279   Tudor, Dean and Tudor, Nancy, comp. Popular Mu-
        sic Periodicals Index. Metuchen, New Jersey:
        Scarecrow Press, 1973- .
        Companion vol. to Armitage and Tudor's An-
        nual Index to Popular Music Record Reviews
        (#118). Early issues comp. by Dean Tudor and
        Andrew Armitage. Published annually, indexes
        articles dealing with popular music in about six-
        ty general and specialized periodicals under vari-
        ous categories. Subject index includes artists;
        author index. Music periodicals indexed include:
        Canadian Composer, Downbeat, English Dance &
        Song, ETHNO, HF, HSR, MusJ, Saturday Review.

280(R) Varley, Douglas H., comp. African Native Music:
        An Annotated Bibliography. Folkstone and Lon-
        don: Dawsons of Pall Mall, 1970. First pub-
        lished in 1936. 116p.

Scope is confined to the Negro and Bantu culture, roughly south of the Sahara. Entries, with
short annotations, are arranged geographically.
Music periodicals indexed include: AMZ, Bul. of
the Folk Song Society of the North East, MQ,
MusAmer, MusCour, Musical Observer, MTNA
Proc, RM, RMI, SIM, ZfMW, ZIM.

281(R) Vierteljahrschrift für Musikwissenschaft.   General-
Register, vols. 1-10, 1885-1894. Ed. by Rudolf
Schwartz. Leipzig: Breitkopf & Härtel, 1895.
Indexed: Author, Name, Subject.

282(R) _____. Index, vols. 1-10, 1885-1894. Ed. by
Friedrich Chrysander and Philipp Spitta. Leipzig:
Breitkopf & Härtel, 1895.
Each vol. has a section "Musicalische Biblio-
graphie" which includes the contents of current
scholarly periodicals in all European languages.

283(R) Vinquist, Mary and Zaslaw, Neal, ed. Performance
Practice: A Bibliography. New York: W. W.
Norton, 1971. 114p. Suppls. in CM, no. 12
(1971), 129-49; CM, no. 15 (1973), 126-36.
Originally in issues of CM, comp. by graduate
students of William S. Newman. Supplements later were comp. and ed. by Thomas W. Baker &
Robert Kline, and by Richard Koprowski and
James Hines. International, with scope and format restrictions Western art music roughly between 1100 and 1900. Thirty-seven music periodicals indexed; also essays and yearbooks.

284(R) Wager, Willis J., comp. Liberal Education and Mu-
sic: A Bibliography. New York: Institute of
Higher Education, Teachers' College, Columbia
University, 1958? 48ℓ.
Divisions: Historical items, General works,
Educational, Professional. Annotated. Music
periodicals indexed: JAMS, MENC, MQ, MusEdJ,
Musica, MM, Juilliard Review.

285(R) Waterman, Richard A., Lichtenwanger, William, et
al., comp. "Bibliography of Asiatic Musics."
NOTES, 5-8, (December 1947-September 1951).
In fifteen installments.
General arrangement is on a geographical-eth-

nological basis. Only sources in European languages are represented (including Russian and
romanized Turkish). 3,488 numbered items are
listed, books, monographs, articles, sections of
larger works, vocal texts, transcriptions of music. The last issue, NOTES, 8/4 (September
1951), is a "Survey of Recordings of Asiatic Music in the United States," with seventy-two items.
An "Ethnic Index" analyzes the contents of the col-
lections in the bibliography. Many music and related periodicals indexed.

286(R) Weisser, Albert. Bibliography of Publications and
Other Resources on Jewish Music. New York:
National Jewish Music Council, 1969. 117p.
Based partly on Joseph Yasser's Bibliography
of Books and Articles on Jewish Music, 1955.
Music periodicals indexed: American Choral Re-
view, American Guild of Organists Quarterly,
American Organist, ARG, C&CG, Journal of
Church Music, JAMS, MQ, MusAmer, MusJ,
OpN, Listener, HF, Stereo Review, etc.

287   Wenk, Arthur B., comp. Analyses of Twentieth-
Century Music, 1940-1970. (Music Library Association Index Series, 13) Ann Arbor, Michigan:
Music Library Association, 1975. 94p.
Provides "rapid access to the hundreds of analytical articles buried in the periodical literature
about newer music." Works by more than 150
composers are indexed in issues of thirty-nine
periodicals and thirty-two monographs. Entries
are arranged by author under each composer.
Scope is international.

288(R) Werner, Jack, comp. "General Bibliography of Books
and Articles on Music." Hinrichsen's Musical
Year Book, 6, (1949/1950), 331-63.
Covers periodicals from January to December
1947. Continues Loewenberg's Bibliography ...
(#211R).

289(R) Williams, David Russell. A Bibliography of the History of Music Theory. 2d ed. New York: Rochester Music Publishers, Inc., 1971. 58p. (3d
ed. in progress.)
Selected theory works and writings intended for

graduate students in theory courses. Part A:
Introductory bibliography; Part B: Theorists and
their treatises, section I: Greek theorists to
Section XXI, Paul Hindemith. Indexes: Treatises,
Names. Music periodicals indexed: AfMW, AM,
JAMS, JRME, MD, MF, M&L, MMR, MQ, MR,
MT, NOTES, RM, SIM, VfMW, ZfMW, etc.

290   Wilson, C. "The Acoustics of Woodwind Instruments;
         A Selected and Annotated Bibliography of Books
         and Articles." Instrum., 9, (April 1955), 14-15.
             Part II: articles from: Instrum., Philosophical
         Magazine and Journal of Science, Journal of the
         Acoustical Society of America, Woodwind Magazine,
         etc.

291(R)   Winick, Steven D. Rhythm: An Annotated Biblio-
         graphy. Metuchen, New Jersey: Scarecrow Press,
         1974. 163p.
             Materials in English, including books, periodi-
         cals, articles and dissertations mostly published
         between 1900 and 1972, pertinent to the general
         background, psychology, and pedagogy of rhythm.
         Annotated, some evaluations. Music periodicals
         indexed: American Organist, Clavier, Etude, In-
         strum., JRME, M&L, MM, MMR, MQ, MT,
         MTNA Proc., MusEdJ, MusAmer, PNA, SchMus,
         Score.

292(R)   Wright, Lesley A., comp. Ed. by Anne Bagnall.
         "Roger Huntington Sessions: A Selective Biblio-
         graphy and a Listing of His Compositions." CM,
         no. 15 (1973), 107-25.
             Music periodicals indexed: Diapason, HF, In-
         ternational Musician, MM, MQ, MusAmer, Mus-
         Cour, NOTES, PNA, MM, etc.

293(R)   Yoo, Yushin, comp. Buddhism: A Subject Index to
         Periodical Articles in English, 1728-1971. Me-
         tuchen, New Jersey: Scarecrow Press, 1973.
         184p.
             With introductory survey of Buddhism, 1,261
         items in about 250 periodicals are indexed under
         subject. Articles are only in English. Author
         and Title indexes. Subject MUSIC is listed under
         ART. Music and related periodicals indexed:
         ETHNO, GSJ, JAF, JIFMC, Musical Review (San

Francisco), SchMus, Spec.

294(R) Zeitschrift der Internationalen Musikgesellschaft.
        Vols. 1-15. Leipzig: Breitkopf & Härtel, 1899-
        1914.
            Index at end of each vol., includes also an in-
        dex to SIM, 1899-1914. Under "Zeitschriftenschau"
        indexes about eighty-four periodicals, mostly mu-
        sical. Vols. 1-11 by author only; vols. 12-15 by
        subject with cross-references from the author.

295(R) Zeitschrift für Musikwissenschaft. Vols. 1-17. Leip-
        zig: Breitkopf & Härtel, 1918-1935.
            Superseded by AMF, 1936-1943, which was su-
        perseded by MF, 1948- . 1914-1918 covered
        retrospectively in 1918, thus following ZIM. In-
        dexes annually all important foreign (some Eng-
        lish and American) periodicals on music in about
        202 journals.

Part VI

BIBLIOGRAPHY OF LISTS OF MUSIC PERIODICALS

296   Albrecht, Otto. "Music periodicals in Germany
1946-1948, " NOTES, 5/4, (Sept. 1948), 494-5.
Follows Frank Campbell's article on European
periodicals (#305R). Gives data on twenty-four
journals, all but two still flourishing in 1948.

297(R)   Apel, Willi, ed. Harvard Dictionary of Music. 2d
ed., rev. & enl. Cambridge, Mass.: Belknap
Press of Harvard University, 1969. 935p.
Under "Periodicals, music," following a short
survey of 18th- and 19th-century periodicals, is
a selected list, classified according to countries,
with a special group of musicological publications.
Reference is also made to the periodicals in the
list of abbreviations, pp. xi-xii.

298(R)   Ayer's Directory of Newspapers and Periodicals.
Philadelphia, Penna.: N. W. Ayer & Sons,
1880- .
Annual, lists about 20,000 newspapers and
periodicals published currently in the United States
and its territories, Canada, Bermuda, Republics
of Panama and the Philippines. Arranged by
states and cities, with indexes. For each periodical included, information is given as to date, frequency of issue, price, circulation, editors, political affiliation, etc.

299(R)   Azhderian, Helen Wentworth, ed. Reference Works
in Music and Music Literature in Five Libraries
of Los Angeles County. Los Angeles: Published
for the Southern California Chapter of the Music
Library Association by the University of Southern
California, 1953. 313p.
"Periodicals and other serial publications, "

pp. 213-39, divided into two sections: English lan-
guage; Other languages.   The five libraries: Hun-
tington Library, San Marino; William Andrews
Clark Library, Los Angeles; Los Angeles Public
Library; University of Southern California, Los
Angeles; University of California, Los Angeles.
Useful compilation, but badly out-of-date, and now
out-of-print.

300(R) Blum, Fred. "East German Music Journals: A
Checklist, " NOTES, 19/3, (June 1962), 399-410.
Intended to supplement James Coover's "Bibliography of East European Music Periodicals"
(#308R).   With few exceptions, current journals in
the field of music are listed.   Of the general music journals, the best coverage of East German
musical activity is in the monthly Musik und Ge-
sellschaft; for scholarly articles of musicological
interest, the quarterly Beiträge zur Musikwissenschaft.   Citations show periodicity, date of first
publications, with holdings of the Library of Congress indicated.

301(R) British Union-Catalogue of Periodicals: A Record of
the Periodicals of the World, From the Seven-
teenth Century to the Present Day, in British
Libraries.   London: Butterworth's Scientific Publications, 1955-1958.   4 vols.   Supplement to
1960.   New York: Academic Press, 1962.
Arranged by title and by organization.   Supplemented since 1964 by a quarterly issue with annual cumulations, picking up new titles to date.

302(R) Camp, William L. and Schwark, Bryan L. Guide to
Periodicals in Education.   2d ed.   Metuchen, New
York: Scarecrow Press, 1975.
Under MUSIC, pp. 343-50, gives title, sub-
scription data, editorial address and policy, manu-
script preparation and disposition, copyright infor-
mation of: AMT, AST, CJ, Clavier, Instrum. ,
JRME, MusEdJ, MusJ, NATS Bul. , Schmus.

303(R) Campbell, Frank C. A Critical Annotated Bibliography of Periodicals.   (American Choral Foundation, Memo no. 33, July 1962) New York: The
American Choral Foundation, Inc. , 1962.   14p.
List directed toward the choral conductor, the

choral singer, the organist. Music for worship
dominates, with some secular music for the chorus
and the organ. Content evaluations of forty-four
music periodicals, giving editor, publisher, address, number of issues, prices, but no date of
first issue.

304(R)   , Eppink, Alice and Fredricks, Jessica.
"Music Magazines of Britain and the United States. "
NOTES, 6/2, (March 1949), 239-62; 6/3, (June
1949), 457-9; 7/3, (June 1950), 372-6.
Compiled by the Music Library Association
Periodicals Committee. Entries arranged in one
alphabet with a broad subject index. Descriptive
annotations. Does not give date of inception.

305(R)   . "Some Current Foreign Periodicals. "
NOTES, 5/2 (March 1948), 189-98.
Tells the wartime fate of many foreign music
periodicals, and a few new ones. Periodicals
cited from France, Netherlands, Belgium, Germany, Portugal, Spain, Latin America, Russia,
England. Supplementary list of additional titles,
p. 198.

306   Clough, F. F. and Cuming, G. J. "Phonographic
Periodicals: A Survey of Some Issued Outside the
United States. " NOTES, 15/4, (September 1958),
537-8.
Originally published in High Fidelity. Journals
devoted exclusively to phonographic matters and
less detailed references to some periodicals giving
some coverage to recorded music. Critical annotations, giving collation, price, publisher, publisher's address, but no date of inception.

307(R)   Collins, Thomas C. , ed. Music Education Materials:
A Selected, Annotated Bibliography Prepared for
the Music Education Research Council of the Music
Educators National Conference. Washington, D. C. :
M. E. N. C. , 1967? 174p.
Periodicals in the field of music education listed, with descriptive annotations; pp. 31-7: audio-
visual periodicals, pp. 153-5: general, film and
film-strips, radio and television, recordings, as-
sociations. Addresses given for music education
materials, pp. 163-74.

308(R)   Coover, James B.   "A Bibliography of East European
         Music Periodicals. "   FAM, 1956, no. 2--1963, no.
         1/2.
             From Bulgaria to Yugoslavia: Part 1, 1956,
         no. 2, pp. 219-26; Part 2, 1957, no. 2, pp. 97-102;
         Part 3, 1958, no. 1, pp. 44-5; Part 4, 1958, no. 2,
         pp. 93-99; Part 5, 1959, no. 1, pp. 27-8; Part 6,
         1960, no. 1, pp. 16-21; Part 7, 1960, no. 2, pp. 69-
         70; Part 8, 1961, no. 2, pp. 75-90; Part 9, 1962,
         no. 2, pp. 78-80.   Index to titles, 1963, no. 1/2,
         pp. 60-71.   List of sources for each country listed,
         followed by a list of periodicals, giving date of
         inception, frequency of issue, publisher, address
         and editor.

309   "Directory of American Music Periodicals. "   Music
         Article Guide, vol. 1/1- .   Winter 1965/1966- 。
             Appears in most issues, giving addresses of
         editors and/or publishers.

310(R)   Fairley, Lee.   "A Check-List of Recent Latin-Amer-
         ican Music Periodicals. "   NOTES, 2/2, (March
         1945), 120-3.
             Annotated list, with full citations.   Includes
         only those periodicals founded since 1940.

311   Gerboth, Walter.   The Music of East and Southeast
         Asia: A Selected Bibliography of Books, Pam-
         phlets, Articles and Recordings.   Albany, New
         York: New York State University, 1963.   23p.
             From review in ETHNO, 8/3, 1964: "arranged
         by nation, a list of over 200 publications and
         seventy-three records with their locations in sev-
         eral New York City libraries indicated. "

312(R)   "German Wartime Music Periodicals. "   NOTES, 5/2,
         (March 1948), 199-206.
             Result of Richard S. Hill's correspondence with
         a German librarian, who wished to remain anony-
         mous.   List based on actual copies received at the
         then Staatsbibliothek Berlin.   Checked and re-
         checked with other sources。   List does not indicate
         political background, nor value, nor significance.
         Changes of title are given; when possible, editor,
         imprint, and serial presentation are given.

313(R)   Grove, Sir George, ed.   Grove's Dictionary of Music
         and Musicians.   5th ed. , ed. by Eric Blom.   Lon-

don: Macmillan; New York: St. Martin's Press,
1954.   9 vols.   Supplement, vol. 10, 1961.
Under "Periodicals, " vol. 6, pp. 637-72, comp.
by A. Hyatt King: Section II: List of periodicals
arranged by countries, in chronological order of
date of appearance and place of publication from
Argentina to Yugoslavia.   Section III: Selective
subject index to the list by country and item, from
Accordion to Zither, including subjects such as
Church Music, Education, Musicology.

314(R)   Heyer, Anna Harriet.   Check-List of Publications of
Music.   Ann Arbor, Michigan: School of Music,
University of Michigan, 1944.   49p.
Music periodicals, pp. 1-10, listed by country
of origin: English, French, German, Italian,
with the holdings of 113 libraries listed by symbols, from California to Wisconsin.

315(R)   Irregular Serials and Annuals: an International Directory: A Classified Guide to Current Foreign
and Domestic Serials, Excepting Periodicals Issued More Frequently Than Once a Year.   3d ed.
New York: Bowker, 1974.   3, 400p.
Companion to Ulrich (# 331R).   Includes 20, 000
important lesser-known publications, with 230 subject areas.   By subjects, with abstracts, indexes,
bibliographies cited under the specific headings.
Title index refers to page giving full citation and
information, with addresses, etc.   Under MUSIC,
pp. 2, 547-73, lists are given of irregularly published publications such as: American Society of
University Composers, Proceedings, giving language of text, date of inception, editor, publisher
whether indexed (cumulative index) and where indexed.

316   Kennington, Donald.   The Literature of Jazz: A
Critical Guide.   London: Library Association,
1970; Chicago: American Library Association,
1971.   142p.
Chapter six, "Periodical Literature, " pp. 91-6,
discusses jazz periodicals under four categories:
those aiming at the widest readership, following
an editorial formula of feature articles, news,
book and record reviews, such as Downbeat, Jazz
Monthly (British), Coda (Canadian); local jazz cov-

erage; discographical magazines; vehicles for buy-
ing and selling of jazz records. An annotated list
of periodicals, pp. 96-103.

317(R) Lindahl, Charles E. "Music Periodicals: New Music
and the Composer (Part 1.)" NOTES, 32/4, (June
1976), 784-93.
List reviewed by the author with purpose "to
present a continuing bibliographical listing of ... a
core research collection of music journals, both
current and retrospective." Includes those which
have ceased publication, preceded by an asterisk.

318(R) _____. "Music Periodicals: Woodwind and Brass."
NOTES, 32/3, (March 1976), 558-66.
Current and retrospective list; titles which have
ceased publication are preceded by an asterisk.
List reviewed by the author.

319   Madsen, Clifford K. and Madsen, Charles H., Jr.
Experimental Research in Music. Englewood
Cliffs, New Jersey: Prentice-Hall, 1970. 116p.
Appendix A: Selected periodicals, pp. 94-8,
lists 153 periodicals, of which nineteen are music
and three related to music. Mostly dealing with
music education. Some of the titles have ceased
publication some years ago. Only the title is
listed.

320   Malm, William P., comp. "A Bibliography of Japanese Magazines and Music." ETHNO, 3, (May
1959), 76-80.
Selected annotated list of twenty-five Japanese
periodicals related to music. In four parts:
Scholarly and popular magazines dealing with tra-
ditional music; Magazines relating to specific tra-
ditional music forms; Magazines concerning Western music; Magazines on dance. Gives Japanese
title, English translation, present editors, city of
origin, frequency of issue, publisher, date of first
publication and price (based on 360 yen to a dol-
lar).

321(R) Musicians' Guide; The Directory of the World of Music. New York: Music Information Service,
1954- .
Vol. for 1972: section of American and foreign

music periodicals listed, giving basic information,
with price. No beginning date or knowledge of
having ceased. United States music periodicals,
pp. 438-57; foreign music periodicals, Argentina-
Yugoslavia, pp. 458-500.

322(R) Die Musik in Geschichte und Gegenwart. Ed. by
Friedrich Blume. Kassel: Bärenreiter, 1949- .
15 vols. and Supplements.
Under "Zeitschriften, " comp. by Imogen Fellinger in vol. 14, columns 1042-1187, 1968: Comprehensive list of music periodicals and serial
publications. Divisions: International; Europe
(Deutschland, pp. 1058-91, Frankreich, pp. 1094-
1114, Grossbritannien und Irland, pp. 1114-23);
Africa (five sections); America: North America
(Canada, United States), Middle America (Costa
Rica, Guatamala, Cuba, Mexico), South America
(six categories), Australia and New Zealand.

323   New Serial Titles; A Union List of Serials Commenc-
ing Publication After December 31, 1949. 3d ed.
Washington, D. C. : Library of Congress, 1961.
2 vols. (1950-1961) 2 vols. (1961-1965) 2 vols.
(1966-1969) 1971- .
Cumulative subject index: Subject Index to New
Serial Titles, 1950-1965. Ann Arbor, Michigan:
Perian Press, 1968.

324(R) "Les Publications Musicales dans le Monde. " RM,
no. 215, 1952, 33-40.
List of music periodicals by country: Alle-
magne-Yugoslavie, giving address only.

325(R) Riedel, A. Répertoire des Périodiques Musicaux
Belges. (Bibliographia Belgica, 8) Bruxelles,
Commision Belge de Bibliographia 1954. 48p.
330 items, periodicals and music serials.

326(R) Riemann, Hugo. Musik-Lexikon. 12. völlig neubear-
beitete Auflage in drei Bänden. Hrsg. von Willi-
bald Gurlitt. Mainz: B. Schott's Söhne, 1959-
1967. 3 vols. Suppl. , Personenteil, vol. 1 & 2.
Hrsg. von Carl Dahlhaus.
Under "Zeitschriften, " vol. 3, pp. 1073-78:
selective list by country.

327(R) Rohlfs, Eckart. Die deutschsprachigen Musikperiodi-
        ca, 1945-1957. (Forschungsbeiträge zur Musik-
        wissenschaft, 11) Regensburg: Gustav Bosse,
        1961. 108p.
        Dissertation, University of Munich, 1957. To
        a certain extent, this expands and supplements the
        list by Freystätter (# 3R). Appendix, pp. 1-115,
        consists of a systematic bibliography of 589 jour-
        nals listed in twelve categories from general, mu-
        sicological, church music, folk music, jazz, to
        music and theater. Included are a chronological
        list and indexes by locality, by title and by name.

        Sheehy, Eugene P. see Winchell, Constance M.

328(R) Standard Periodical Directory. 4th ed. , ed. by Leon
        Garry. New York: Oxbridge Publishing Co. ,
        1973- .
        Published irregularly (the 3d ed. was issued in
        1969) supplements Ayer (# 298R) and Ulrich (# 331R).
        Lists periodicals of the United States and Canada
        under subject or field of interest, with an index
        to titles. Comprehensive in scope. Music sub-
        jects as: Music and Music Trades, Research in
        Music Education, etc. give information: address,
        telephone, short comment on type, price, but does
        not give date of inception nor whether it has
        ceased.

329(R) Svobodova, Marie. "Music Journals in Bohemia and
        Moravia, 1796-1970. " FAM, 19/1/2, (January-
        August 1972), 22-41.
        Includes those written in Czech as well as those
        in German "in a Czech spirit" which were forc-
        runners of the later Czech musical journals. Es-
        pecially noted is the AMZ (Leipzig) 1798-1848).
        Complete data is given as much as possible; des-
        criptive notes often in English with most of the
        Czech titles translated into English. 259 items
        cited. There is a convenient chronological regis-
        ter, pp. 38-41.

330(R) _____, and Potúcek, Juraj. "Music Journals in
        Slovakia, 1871-1970. " FAM, 21/1/2, (January-
        August 1974), 32-36.
        With this and the above article, attempt is made
        to present an overall review of periodicals from

the territory of the Czechoslovak Socialist Repub-
lic. List of twenty-seven titles with a short bibliography of sources and a chronological register
giving the item number of the title, pp. 35-36.

331(R) Ulrich, Carolyn. Ulrich's International Periodicals
        Directory: A Classified Guide to a Selected List
        of Current Periodicals. 16th ed. Ann Arbor,
        Michigan: Bowker, 1975/1976. Annual supple-
        ment.
        A comprehensive list of 57,000 periodicals,
        with 250 subject headings arranged under sections:
        scientific, technical, medical publications; the
        arts, humanities, social sciences, business. Sub-
        section on MUSIC gives full title, first year, fre-
        quency, price, publisher, address. It indicates
        abstracts, book reviews, bibliographies, illustra-
        tions, and states whether the journal is indexed,
        how and where. Cross-references to such as:
        Art-General, Bibliographies, Folklore, Sound Re-
        cording and Reproduction, Theater, etc.

332(R) Union List of Serials in Libraries of the United
        States and Canada. 3d ed. New York: H. W.
        Wilson, 1965. 5 vols.
        To be used with New Serial Titles (#323).
        Lists both current and extinct periodicals, giving
        dates and place of publication, with international
        coverage. Arranged by title and organization.
        Location of periodicals and other serial publica-
        tions is given for all participating North American
        libraries, including the Library of Congress.

333(R) Watanabe, Ruth T. "Current Periodicals for Music
        Libraries." NOTES, 23/2, (December 1966),
        225-35.
        Purpose of article is to identify the chief cur-
        rent periodicals in music for possible purchase by
        the small library, the medium or average library,
        the large music library. Lists are arranged under
        categories: Current-Events, Learned Journals,
        Journals of Music Education and Pedagogy, Audio
        Magazines, Journals of Performing Media, Church-
        Music Journals, "New Music" Journals, Promotion-
        al or Propaganda Journals, Non-Music Journals.
        Full citations are given, including price, but no
        dates of inception. Descriptive annotations for
        each title.

334(R)   Wiegand, J. J.   "A List of State Music Education
         Periodicals in the United States." JRME, 1,
         (Fall 1953), 135-9.
             List alphabetically by state, from Arizona to
         Wyoming.   Most of them described in detail.

335(R)   Winchell, Constance M.   Guide to Reference Books.
         9th ed., by Eugene P. Sheehy.   Chicago: Amer-
         ican Library Association, 1976.
             Standard and indispensable guide to general
         bibliography.   Includes a large section on music,
         code number BH, which lists books in categories:
         General Works (Guides), Bibliographies (Books,
         Current, Periodicals, Dissertations, Manuscripts
         and Published Music, Indexes, Encyclopedias,
         Biographical Dictionaries, History, etc.).

ABBREVIATIONS

ACA	American Composers Alliance, Bulletin, 1951-
AfMW	Archiv für Musikwissenschaft, 1917-27; 1952-
AM	Acta Musicologica, 1928-
AMF	Archiv für Musikforschung, 1936-43 (Supersedes ZfMW)
AMS	American Musicological Society, Bul., 1936-48, Papers 1936-41
AMT	American Music Teacher, 1951
AMZ	Allgemeine musikalische Zeitung, 1798-1848; 1863-65; 1866-82
ARG	American Record Guide, May 1935-
AST	American String Teacher, 1951-
Aufl.	Auflage
Ausg.	Ausgabe
Bd.	Band (Volume)
BQ	Brass Quarterly, 1957-64; Brass and Woodwind Quarterly, 1966-69
Bul.	Bulletin
C&CG	Choral and Organ Guide, 1947-1970
ca., c.	Circa (About)
CJ	Choral Journal, May 1959-

Clavier   Clavier, March/April 1962-

CM   Current Musicology, Spring 1965-

Comp.   Compiler(s), Compiled

D (#)   Duckles, Vincent. Music Reference and Re-
                 search Materials, 1974

DM   Die Musik, 1901-15

Ed.   Editor, Edition, Edited, Edited By

Enl.   Enlarged

Et al.   Et alii (and others)

ETHNO   Ethnomusicology, 1953- (Ethnomusicology
                 Newsletter, 1953-57)

FAM   Fontes Artis Musicae, 1954-

GSJ   Galpin Society Journal, 1948-

HF   High Fidelity, 1951-

Hft.   Heft

Hrsg.   Herausgegeben

HSR   Hi Fi/Stereo Review, 1949-

Instrum.   Instrumentalist, 1946-

JAAC   Journal of Aesthetics and Art Criticism,
                 1941-

JAF   Journal of American Folklore, 1888-

JAMS   Journal of the American Musicological Society,
                 1948-

JIFMC   Journal of the International Folk Music Coun-
                 cil, 1949-

JMP   Jahrbuch der Musikbibliothek Peters, 1895-
                 1941

JMT   Journal of Music Therapy, 1964-

JoMT   Journal of Music Theory, 1957-

JRB   Journal of Renaissance and Baroque Music,
               1946-47; Musica Disciplina, 1947-

JRME   Journal of Research in Music Education,
               1953-

M&L   Music and Letters, 1920-

MA   Musical Antiquary, 1909-13

MD   Musica Disciplina, 1946- see JRB

MENC   Music Educators' National Conference, Year-
               book, 1907-40

MF   Die Musikforschung, 1948- (Supersedes AMF)

MfMG   Monatshefte für Musikgeschichte, 1869-1905

MM   Modern Music, 1924-46; League of Composers'
               Review, 1924-Apr. 1925

MMR   Monthly Musical Record, 1871-1960

MO   Musical Opinion, 1877-

MQ   Musical Quarterly, 1915-

MR   Music Review, 1940-

MS   Music Survey, 1947-June 1952

MT   Musical Times, 1844-

MTNA Proc.   Music Teachers' National Association, Pro-
               ceedings, 1876-1946

MusAmer   Musical America, 1898-1964; Hi/Fi & MusAmer,
               1965-

MusCour   Musical Courier, 1880-1962

MusEdJ   Music Educators' Journal, 1914- (Music Super-

visors' Bulletin, 1914-March 1915; Music
Supervisors' Journal, Apr. 1915-Aug. 1934)

MusJ   Music Journal, 1943-

N. No(s)   Number(s)

N. D.   No Date

N. P.   No Place

NATS Bul   National Association of Teachers of Singing,
                Bulletin, 1944-

NHQ   New Hungarian Quarterly, 1960-

NMZ   Neue Musik-Zeitung, 1880-1928

NOTES   Music Library Association, Notes, ser. 1,
                n. 1-15, July 1934-December 1942; ser. 2
                n. 1, December 1943-

NZfM   Neue Zeitschrift für Musik, 1834-

OpN   Opera News, 1936-

p. pp.   Page, Pages

PMA   Proceedings of the Royal Musical Association,
                1874-

PNA   Perspectives of New Music, 1962-

Pseud.   Pseudonym

RaM   La Rassegna Musicale, 1928-43; 1947-62

RBM   Revue Belge de Musicologie, 1946-

RdM   Revue de Musicologie, 1922- (Preceded by
                Bulletin de la Société Française de Musi-
                cologie, 1917-21; 3 vols. appeared under
                title: Société Française de Musicologie,
                Rapports et Communications. References
                are made by year and page, vol. no. is
                inconsistent)

RenN	Renaissance News, Spring, 1948-
Rev.	Revised, Revised By, Revision
RM	La Revue Musicale, 1920-
RMI	Rivista Musicale Italiana, 1894-1955
SchMus	School Musician, 1929-
Ser.	Series
SFQ	Southern Folklore Quarterly, 1937-
SIM	Sammelbände der Internationalen Musikgesellschaft, 1899-1914
SMZ	Schweizerische Musikzeitung, 1961-
Spec	Speculum, 1926-
Suppl.	Supplement
SZMW	Studien zur Musikwissenschaft, Beihefte der Denkmäler der Tonkunst in Österreich, 1913-34, 1955-
VfMW	Vierteljahrschrift für Musikwissenschaft, 1885-94
Vol. (s)	Volume(s)
ZfMW	Zeitschrift für Musikwissenschaft, 1918-35
ZIM	Zeitschrift der Internationalen Musikgesellschaft, 1899-1914

ANNOTATED SELECTED BIBLIOGRAPHY

Barton, Mary N. and Bell, Marion V., comp. Reference Books: A Brief Guide. 7th ed. Baltimore, Maryland: Enoch Pratt Free Library, 1970. 158p.
Aim is to "present some of the salient points in regard to the more generally useful and popular reference materials." Annotations are factual as well as descriptive. Of use to the bibliography are "Biographical Dictionaries and Indexes" pp. 20-1; "Indexes to Magazines," "Lists of Magazines," "Book Reviews," pp. 36-43; "Reference Books in Special Subjects: The Humanities," pp. 60-138.

Christopher, Edna L. A Study of the Indexing of Periodical Literature in the Field of Music, 1954. Thesis, M.A., Graduate Library School, University of Chicago, March 1959. 63p.
The retrospective music periodical indexing project of 1938 is noted. Covering the period 1949-1954, the indexing policies and practices of the Music Index (1949-) are discussed as to completeness, reviews (treatment of books, music, periodicals) and a comparison is made as to duplication of coverage between the Music Index and the H. W. Wilson indexes: Readers' Guide, International Index, Art Index, and Education Index. Her conclusion: for complete coverage, both the Music Index and the general Wilson indexes need to be consulted.

Duckles, Vincent H. Music Reference and Research Materials: An Annotated Bibliography. 3d ed. New York: The Free Press, 1974. 526p.
Pertinent to the bibliography is the chapter on "Bibliographies of Music Literature" pp. 128-87, which lists, with short, descriptive annotations, monographs and periodical articles from general to special fields, including current items. Practical and useful: the Subject Index, pp. 470-80.

Kujoth, Jean Spealman. Subject Guide to Periodical Indexes
    and Review Indexes. Metuchen, New Jersey: Scare-
    crow Press, 1969. 129p.
        Two parts: 1) "Academic-Subject Index, " lists
    titles of periodical indexes under broad subjects;
    letter symbols refer to the "Type-of-Information
    Code" such as AIP (indexes articles in periodicals),
    RRP (indexes reviews of phonorecords), etc.   2)
    Lists the indexes by title and describes each one by:
    Form, Content, Subjects.   In Part 1, under the sub-
    ject MUSIC are thirteen references, with cross-ref-
    erences to Area Studies, Dance, Theatre Arts.

Mixter, Keith E.   General Bibliography for Music Research.
    (Detroit Studies in Music Bibliography, 33) 2d ed.
    Detroit, Information Coordinators, 1975.   135p.
        An augmented revision of the first edition, 1962.
    Purpose, in general, "to explore only non-music
    titles. " Of particular interest to the bibliography is
    Chapter VIII, Indexes and Directories: "Periodical
    and Newspaper Indexes" and "Book Reviews. "

Solow, Linda, comp. A Checklist of Music Bibliographies
    and Indexes in Progress and Unpublished. (Music
    Library Association Index Series, 3) 3d ed.   Ann
    Arbor, Michigan: Music Library Association, 1974.
    40p.
        273 entries in this edition.   Part I: Listed by
    compiler, by institution, giving titles and such infor-
    mation as address of author, description of the work
    (state of completion, scope, indexes, size, format)
    and statement of availability.   "To be published" is
    noted.   Part II: Index of Subjects (under broad cate-
    gories), Proper and Place Names, titles mentioned
    within the entries.   Items included within the biblio-
    graphy: nos. 124R, 173R, 199R, 201, 212, 260R (in
    the 2d ed.), and Toy (listed below).

Toy, Jacquelyn G.   Sources of Music Periodical Indexing: A
    Bibliography of English and German Language Music
    Periodicals Indexed Before 1949. Research Report
    Submitted to the Kent State University School of Li-
    brary Science for the Degree of M. L. S. , August
    1949.   21p.   Typescript.
        Points out the dearth of indexing for music peri-
    odicals before the Music Index of 1949, but that many
    music periodicals have been analyzed in the more

general periodical indexes.   Thirty-two English language and sixty-six German language periodicals
which were indexed before 1949 were examined.   The
period covered: 1804-1949.   The indexes were: Annual Library Index, 1908-1910; Annual Literary Index,
1908-1910, and the following indexes appearing in the
bibliography: nos. 33R, 35, 36R, 37R, 38R, 49R, 54R,
104R.   Not annotated.   Available for xeroxing.

Watanabe, Ruth W.   Introduction to Music Research.   Englewood Cliffs, New Jersey: Prentice-Hall, 1967.
237p.
        Pertinent to the bibliography are sections of
"Periodicals, " pp. 91-103, in particular the listing
and discussion of current and retrospective periodical
indexes, the survey of contemporary music periodicals and current non-musical journals, also the bibliographies at the end of each chapter.   A useful complementary volume to Duckles (listed above).

INDEX OF AUTHORS, EDITORS, AND COMPILERS

(All references are to item numbers in the bibliography; the addition of an "R" indicates that the title indexes music articles appearing before 1949, retrospectively.)

INDEX OF SUBJECTS

INDEX OF TITLES